RUNSPIRATIONS

Amazing Stories,
Timeless Wisdom,
and Motivational Quotes
To Help You Run Stronger
Every Day

by Amby Burfoot
&
Gail Waesche Kislevitz

Illustrations by Patrick Regan

First edition

ISBN: 978-1711655994

Book design: Y42K Publishing Services
https://www.y42k.com/publishing-services/

Table of Contents

ACKNOWLEDGEMENTS

I want to thank every runner I have ever known in my 52 years of picking up this sport, from my running soul mates to the casual runner I pass on the streets and trails and exchange the runner nod. That nod is the secret we runners share, knowing that something amazing is going to happen when we step out the door to take a run.

I've been fortunate to have runners in my life who have taught me, mentored me and nurtured me. Toshiko d'Elia, Grete Waitz, Young John Kelley and others gave me their sound advice. They live on in my head and heart.

Like many runners profiled on these pages, I plan to run forever and keep discovering new things about our sport and continue to be Runspired!

—Gail Kislevitz

My first teachers were the most important ones, as I had so much to learn. Special thanks then to John J. Kelley, Charley "Doc" Robbins, Hal Higdon, Jeff Galloway, John A. Kelley, and Ted Corbitt.

Dave Costill, Paul Thompson, Tim Noakes, and Steve Blair lured me into the science of running, which has been a lifelong interest.

Runners don't just like to run; they also like to talk about running. In doing so, they share their passion, and spread valuable information to others.

So, runners: Keep running, keep talking, and keep sharing. You are the original social media.

—Amby Burfoot

INTRODUCTION

Hello. Let us introduce ourselves. We are Amby Burfoot and Gail Kislevitz, two lifetime runners and writers who enjoy sharing their passion for running and health with others.

Together, we have finished more than 100 marathons and covered more than 200,000 miles. Amby has won the Boston Marathon (1968) and is still running it (2018). Gail has completed all six World Marathon Majors, achieving her final star at Tokyo in 2019. (Learn more about us at the end of this book.)

We've written this book, RUNSPIRATIONS, because we believe that personal motivation/inspiration is the runner's most important tool. Not your heart size. Not your leg length. Not your vo2 max. Not your diet.

Every run begins in your mind and is nourished by your thoughts. There's no escaping it: You run as you think.

We're not Pollyannas. We know that everyone has bad days, everyone gets older, everyone gets slower. On bad days, you might be tempted to quit. That's why we wrote RUNSPIRATIONS. We don't want you to quit. We don't want you to lose all the physical and emotional benefits of running.

The only way to keep on keeping on is to stay motivated. Or, to put it another way, motivation is every runner's job 1. Not running more hills. Not stretching. Not eating more veggies (though that's a good idea). But keeping your motivation on full.

We think this book can help.

Every runner we know feels inspired by stories of other amazing runners--from Olympic champions to weight-loss winners to 80-year-olds who are still pushing back the barriers.

We all seek timeless wisdom that will help us enjoy every run while minimizing mistakes. We enjoy motivational quotes from runners, writers, leaders, and philosophers--quotes that reveal deep truisms and guide us to clear action steps.

So that's what we have pulled together in RUNSPIRATIONS: great stories, great advice, and great quotes.

This book is suitable for runners of all ages. The young will discover personalities, insights, and motivation to spark their daily workouts.

Midlife runners already know about human biology and aging. Here they will see the value of continuing to run and stay fit. You can make no better investment.

What's the best term for senior runners? Masters? Veterans? Old farts? It makes no difference to us. We just want you to remember that your quality of life can only be sustained by quality exercise.

We fully agree with the popular saying: "It's not about the years in your life; it's about the life in your years." And the best way to support that life is not with a fist full of prescription meds but a head full of powerful motivations.

Cultivate your runspirations. Every. Single. Day.

This isn't a book that needs to be read front to back, page by page. Quite the opposite. You can dip in wherever you want. On every page, you'll find new and different runspirations.

RUNSPIRATIONS is a book you should never finish reading. That's not our egos speaking. It's our belief that you will find new meaning each and every time you re-read these pages. Our friends have told us that, and we think it will apply to you, also.

This book will prove especially helpful when you hit low points in your life and running. So keep it nearby, and ready to serve. It might take just five minutes, or less.

And those minutes could make a lifetime of difference. As Rudyard Kipling wrote, "If you can fill the unforgiving minute / With sixty seconds worth of distance run...."

AMAZING STORIES

Ever since Pheidippides made his historic and probably-fictional run from the Plains of Marathon to downtown Athens, we runners have enjoyed reading tales of great effort and purpose. Pheidippides fought with the city's great warriors to repel the invading Persians, then ran roughly 26 miles to alert Athens's women, children, and elders.

"Rejoice. Victory is ours." They may have been Pheidippides' last words, but they were glorious ones. The Athenian victory preserved many of humankind's greatest cultural advances: democracy, a legal system, philosophy, mathematics, drama, the arts, and more.

The first great runners were military men, but the field has grown immensely since then. In fact, one of running's greatest achievements has been the way it stretched out its arms to welcome everyone. Wartime heroes, and also peacetime Olympians. Men, and also women. The able-bodied, and also the physically challenged. The young, and also the old.

In the following pages, you'll read amazing stories from each of the above groups. These runners enrich our sport. Their courage makes us all a little braver.

ANNE AUDAIN: Clubfeet to Fast Feet

Anne Audain wanted to be like the other kids in her school but she had one major problem. She was born with clubfeet. Instead of playing she suffered throughout her childhood with bone deformities in both feet. When she was 13 she underwent reconstructive surgery and started high school in her native New Zealand with customized recovery boots instead of fashionable teenage shoes.

"I wanted to be like all the other kids in my neighborhood," recalls Audain. A fierce competitor emerged. By age 15 she was running cross-country and at 17 qualified for the 1972 Munich Olympics in the 1500m. Over the course of her career she would qualify for a total of six Olympic games in every distance from the 800m to the marathon and set a world record in the 5000m.

She immigrated to the US in 1985 and became a citizen in 1995. After retiring from professional running Audain became an elementary school teacher, inspiring her students with a "can-do" attitude. She also fought for women's rights to receive prize money that cost her a temporary lifetime ban from the sport in 1981 when she accepted prize money.

Audain did not let a birth deformity hold her back from realizing her dreams of becoming a professional runner. She has been honored by Queen Elizabeth ll and inducted into the Running USA Hall of Fame, the New Zealand Sports Hall of Fame, and the RRCA Distance Hall of Fame.

ROGER BANNISTER: First runner to break 4 minutes in the mile

In 1954, Roger Bannister faced perhaps the most difficult running challenge of all time: He wanted to run under 4 minutes for the one-mile. But many doctors and exercise scientists proclaimed a sub-4:00 mile physically impossible. The heart would explode first, they said. Or perhaps the lungs would implode. Everyone agreed that any serious attempt at a sub-4 mile carried multiple risks.

That's why progress came so slowly. The Finn, Paavo Nurmi, broke 4:10 in 1923. The Swedes dropped from 4:06 to 4:01 in the early 1940s. Then … a complete stall. No one could run faster. It appeared a human physiologic limit had been reached.

In 1952, Bannister was favored to win an Olympic gold medal in the 1500 meters. However, he ran poorly, failing to make the final. Discouraged by this Olympic result, he realized he had only one other alternative: the sub-4-mile.

On May 6, 1954, at a track near Oxford, the determined medical student finally achieved the impossible. With perfect pacing from friends Chris Brasher and Chris Chataway, he concluded the first three laps in 3:01. Then he began sprinting.

"Those last few seconds seemed never-ending," he wrote in his memoir. "The arms of the world were waiting to receive me if only I reached the tape without slackening my speed. I leapt at the tape like a man taking his last spring from the chasm that threatens to engulf him." He finished in 3:59.4.

GAYLE BARRON: First woman of Southern running, and Boston Marathon champ

Fifty years ago almost no one in the South ran long distances. The weather was bad, and the culture worse--too football-centric. If you happened to be a woman in the South, well, forget about running!

Gayle Barron grew up in this era, learned the prevailing code--put ribbons in your hair, join the cheerleading squad--and somehow broke free. She ran long and fast. In 1971, when her husband said he was going to run Atlanta's first big 10K, the now famous Peachtree Race on July 4th, she said, "Me, too!" And then she won the women's division.

Several years later, the same husband said he was going to run a marathon. "Me, too!" said Gayle. And she won again. Soon she met a small group of Atlanta men who trained for and raced the Boston Marathon every April. She joined them for weekend long runs over Atlanta's infamous hills.

That made the Boston hills seem easy. In 1978, Barron became the first (and to date, only) Southern woman to win the Boston Marathon. She broke the tape in 2:44:52, a personal record. Some criticized her for the ribbons in her hair. Why try to be pretty? "My mother taught me to always dress well," she replied. "What's the problem?"

More importantly, she followed a path that felt right to her. "I started from nothing, but I stuck with the training," she says. "That's how you achieve anything--with patience and consistency."

BEN BEACH: Boston Marathon's longest "streaker" overcomes nerve disease

Like many Harvard College freshman in 1968, Ben Beach was looking for something a bit wacky to do. Only he skipped the "sex, drugs, and rock n roll," and wandered much farther off the beaten track. On April 19, 1968, he found his way to Hopkinton, MA, and followed about 1000 runners to the Boston Marathon start line. "I was completely unprepared," he says. "I had no idea how to train for a marathon."

Nonetheless, he managed to finish 3:23:50. The next April, he headed to Hopkinton again, and the next, and the next, and the.... By 2019, Beach had strung together the longest consecutive finish streak in Boston Marathon history--52 in a row, and counting.

Through the years, he has run as fast 2:27:26 (1981) and as slow as 6 hours. But he's never let anything get in the way of his annual Hopkinton to Boston trek. Beach's performances tailed off significantly after he was diagnosed with dystonia in 2002. It's a rare neurological disease that causes his leg muscles not to "hear" his brain. He tells his legs to run, but sometimes they don't listen, and they refuse to operate as requested. Result: A severe "hitch" or limp in his stride.

Still, Beach pushes onward. "I had no sense in 1968 that I'd be running the Boston Marathon for life, but now it's a big part of me," he says. "It's a challenge that keeps me going."

DICK BEARDSLEY: He suffered some terrible accidents, but still enjoys every run

Like many runners, Dick Beardsley had a low-key start to his marathon career. Unlike others, Beardsley soared to world-class fame, then encountered terrifying obstacles. Through it all, he maintained a zestful, positive outlook.

Raised on a Minnesota dairy farm, Beardsley ran his first marathon in 1977--a 2:47. He then improved in each of his next 12 marathons, landing himself in the Guinness Book of World Records. By the end of 1981, he had dropped his best time into the 2:09s.

However, no one thought he had a chance against marathon titan Alberto Salazar in the 1982 Boston Marathon. No one, that is, but Beardsley himself. He led nearly every step of the way in the famous "Duel in the Sun" until Salazar outsprinted him at the end.

"If the race had been 50 meters longer, I'm not sure either of us would have finished," Beardsley said afterwards. Salazar was so impressed that he pulled Beardsley up onto the victory stand beside him.

Later in life, Beardsley suffered several horrific accidents on heavy farm machinery, had multiple back and knee surgeries, and at one point was arrested for forging pain killer medicine prescriptions. With time at treatment centers, he got clean and returned to Minnesota to run a B & B and fishing-guide business. "Even though I'm now slower than molasses in January, I enjoy my running as much as ever," he says. "I go to bed every night looking forward to the next morning's run."

MARILYN BEVANS: First African American woman marathoner

Marilyn Bevans thought she would win her first track race in Baltimore in1961. She was black, all the other girls white. Bevans figured she would break the tape like Wilma Rudolph, winner of the previous year's Olympic 100 meters. Instead, she finished last, and says, "I learned right away that I wasn't a sprinter."

So she turned to longer distances. Only problem: There was no track team for her in high school or college. It wasn't until her grad school days at Springfield (MA) College that she met other distance runners. They introduced her to local road races costing 50 cents to enter. Most of the time she was the only black runner. Always, she was the only black woman. Sometimes she was the first female finisher.

One summer she met other runners from the Baltimore Road Runners Club. Bevans fell in with them, and discovered a whole new world—the marathon world. "I was a good listener, and did what they said," she remembers. "My runs got longer and longer."

This path took her inevitably to the Boston Marathon. Even there, she was again the only black woman. In 1974, she finished her first Boston in 3:17. In 1977, she was second overall in 2:51:12. Two years later she dropped under the 2:50 barrier with a 2:49:56. She also won the Baltimore Marathon twice. "Running is such a healthy, positive activity," she says. "It gives you peace, quiet, and a time for thinking. But it also makes you tough. You learn to achieve things."

ABEBE BIKILA: From rural Ethiopia to worldwide marathon glory

Abebe Bikila grew up in rural, high-altitude Ethiopia, and joined his country's Imperial Guard at age 20. A Swedish track coach was hired to oversee the Guard's conditioning programs. The coach soon noticed that Bikila could run almost without fatigue, so he trained him for the 1960 Rome Olympic Marathon.

In Rome, Bikila tried running shoes for the first time in his life. Hated them. He was so much more comfortable running barefoot. No matter that the Rome course included a long stretch over the ancient, rock-hard Appian Way. On the start line, one European marathoner looked at the barefoot Bikila, and commented to a teammate: "There's one runner we don't have to worry about."

Wrong. Bikila surged to the front after 24 miles, and broke the tape in 2:15:16.2--an Olympic and World record. Four years later at the Tokyo Olympics, Bikila cruised (this time in shoes) to a four-minute victory. He ran 2:12:11—another new world record. In 1968, he attempted the unthinkable "threepeat" in Mexico City, but was stopped midrace by a leg injury. At that point, he turned to teammate Mamo Wolde, and instructed Wolde to win, which he did.

Bikila's life came to a tragic end in 1973, several years after he was paralyzed in a car accident. Distance runners around the world still honor him for the way he left East Africa as an unknown, and totally dominated the marathon world. He is often referred to as, "Abebe the lion hearted."

BRIAN BOYLE: Crushed under a car, he survived and became an Ironman

Completing an Ironman event (2.4-mile swim, 112 bike ride and a 26.2 marathon) is tough enough, but to complete one after dying on the operating table – eight times - and being brought back, let's just say that's staggering.

On July 6, 2004, 18-year old Brian Boyle was returning home when a dump truck smashed into his Camaro, crushing his pelvis, ribs, and pushing his heart to the right side of his chest. Both lungs collapsed. He lost 60 percent of his blood, endured 14 surgeries and 36 blood transfusions. After spending two months in a coma and losing 100 pounds, Boyle, a former body-builder and state-champion swimmer from Welcome, Maryland, could barely blink his eyes. Doctors predicted that if he survived he might not be able to walk again.

When he awoke from the coma, he heard the word "vegetable" and knew he had to somehow claw his way back to the living. Three and a half years later Boyle completed the Ironman World Championships. He has also completed nine marathons and one 50-miler.

Boyle's story of surviving a gruesome tragedy through sheer will and determination has been described in his book, Iron Heart. He was recognized by President Barack Obama as a "Champion of Change." He is also a spokesperson for the American Red Cross. Boyle believed in himself and never gave up, characteristics of a true fighter.

CHERYL BRIDGES (Treworgy): First woman to break 2:50 in the marathon

Cheryl Pedlow wanted to run, but not to attract attention. As a high schooler in Indianapolis, IN, she only wanted to lose a few pounds. She pulled on a thick hoodie before beginning her laps on the track. Why should anyone be bothered by her presence?

But they were. In fact, the Board of Education convened a special meeting to discuss this unexpected new issue--girls and running. The Board decided Pedlow was okay, so long as she stayed away from the boys' athletic fields. That way, she wouldn't "distract" them.

Pedlow found a supportive coach. In 1965, he took her to the National Women's Cross-Country meet in Boston in 1965. She was 17. On the start line, she thought, "This is so scary. I don't know what I'm doing." She finished a strong seventh.

Six years later, living in California as Mrs. Cheryl Bridges, she decided to enter the 1971 Western Hemispheres Marathon--her second attempt at the distance. The first had turned into "a death march the last 10 miles." This time she was ready.

Trained and steely fit, Bridges covered the distance in 2:49:50--a new women's world record. "The marathon was an opportunity to spread my wings and challenge myself," she says.

[Footnote: Bridges's daughter, Shalane Flanagan, made three U.S. Olympic teams. She won a silver medal in the 2008 Beijing Olympics 10,000, and won the 2017 New York City Marathon. Like mother, like daughter.]

GRACE BUTCHER: Pioneer 800-meter runner

Grace Butcher badly wanted to be a great runner. As a child, she wrote "FOS" at the bottom of notes to friends. The letters stood for "Future Olympic Star." She placed posters of famous milers like Glenn Cunningham on her bedroom wall. Only one problem: She was born too early, in 1934, and grew up in rural Ohio, far from any youth track clubs. Nobody believed girls could run a mile.

In high school, she asked her school principal to start a girls' team. Nope, not going to happen. Her mother finally located a team in distant Cleveland. There, the girls only ran sprints. How about a mile? Butcher asked. "There's no mile for women," she was told. "The longest distance is 200 meters."

In her 20s, Butcher gave up the competitive running dream, married, and had two children. Things finally changed when a women's 800 was added to the 1960 Rome Olympics schedule. She started training again, and won the national championship in 1959. The next year she trained as much as three times a day for the Olympic Trials. Too much. She got injured.

Butcher ran the Trials anyway, finishing in the middle of the pack. She later gained a PhD in English Literature, landed a professorship, and entered masters competitions in the 1970s and beyond. "I developed a life motto," she says. "'Keep on moving on.' We're all here to discover our life's purpose. Once we do, for Heaven's sake, get on with it!"

JULIA CHASE: America's first woman road racer

Julia Chase wouldn't take "No" as an answer. Though just 18, she had traveled to the 1961 Manchester Road Race (5 miles) with several running idols, including two-time Olympic marathon runner John J. Kelley. The guys knew she could cover five miles, and she knew it too.

But race organizers refused to let her enter. They said Amateur Athletic Union rules wouldn't allow a woman to run longer than 880 yards. Chase had listened politely to this argument the previous year. She stood on the sidelines and watched. But not this year.

With photographers from LIFE magazine and other national media snapping away, Chase dodged around race organizers, and took off after the male runners. "The officials were just fat, old guys who couldn't move very fast," she recalls. "No problem."

Chase ran strongly the whole way, completing the course at a more-than-respectable 7:10 pace. "I was jubilant at the end," she says. "I was doing cartwheels on the sidewalk." The New York Times reported: "All the women went the distance. Two of the men failed to finish."

Chase later gained a PhD in zoology, and did field work with bats and chimpanzees. She appeared on "Sesame Street" as Batlady. At midcareer, she entered medical school and achieved an M.D. with an emphasis on psychiatry. There seemed little she couldn't accomplish. "Running puts you in touch with your deepest resolve," she says. "You learn that you don't have to do conventional things. You can do whatever feels worthwhile to you."

MARKO CHESTO: Kenya to Alaska, frostbite amputee to Boston Marathon

Not many students from Kenya, with an average temperature of 85 degrees, would accept a transfer to Alaska where winter temperatures can drop to minus 50. Marko Chesto did just that when he accepted a track scholarship to the University of Alaska in Anchorage in 2008 and quickly earned All-American status.

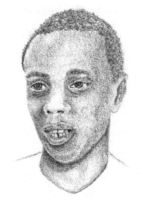

His life changed in an instant when he went out for a run on a winter day in 2011, got lost and spent three days wandering in the woods where the temperature dipped to single digits and snowed more than a foot. His shoes were frozen to his feet. Suffering severe frostbite, doctors amputated both his feet about six inches from the knee.

He was fitted with prosthetics three weeks after the surgery.

A few months after the amputation he slowly started running, eventually entering local races where he walked and jogged. He also got married and had three kids. In 2018 he moved his family to Florida where he could train year-round on running blades donated by the Challenged Athletes Foundation. He ran the 2019 Boston Marathon in 2:42:24, the fastest-ever time by a double amputee.

"The fans along the course were amazing and really cheered me on," states Chesto. "I could not have done it without their support."

Chesto took chances in life that may have seemed risky but he showed great fortitude with the destiny he was dealt.

TED CORBITT: Grandson of slaves and pioneer distance runner

Ted Corbitt (1939-2007), a grandson of slaves, defied racism and discrimination for most of his life to become an Olympian, the First Father of Distance Running, and a world-renowned physical therapist. He was an example of excellence on and off the track, a man of true dignity.

Corbitt began running as a child in South Carolina but from the beginning 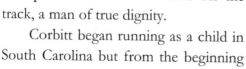 was faced with racism. At the University of Cincinnati where he ran the 880, mile, and 2-mile, racial discrimination followed him wherever he went. When track meets were held in the Midwest, he had to stay separate from his teammates and eat at "colored only" restaurants. In the 70s, the police constantly stopped him when he ran to work in his street clothes.

He was the first African American to represent the US in the 1952 Olympic marathon in Helsinki, the first president of New York Road Runners (1958) and held the record for running the most sub-three-hour finishes at Boston (19).

In all, he ran 199 marathons and ultra-marathons. He ran 200-mile weeks. He would run a 31-mile loop around Manhattan and if he was feeling really good, he'd do it again. His highest monthly training mileage was 1,002.5 in July of 1969 at age 50. He remained a full-time therapist into his 80s and at 82 walked 303 miles in a six-day race.

As a physical therapist, no one came close to his skills, his research or his understanding of how the body works. But more than his many records and awards, Corbitt is best remembered for being a kind human being. He died in 2007 at the age of 88.

GLEN CUNNINGHAM: A fire destroyed his legs, but he went to two Olympics

Glenn Cunningham was an 8-year old Kansas youth attending a wooden schoolhouse near Elkhart when an explosion and fire destroyed the school. His brother Floyd, 13, was killed in the fire, and Cunningham's legs were badly burned. He had no flesh remaining over his knees and shins, and lost all the toes on his left foot.

In fact, his doctors thought he would never walk again. They recommended amputation. However, Cunningham protested so strongly that his parents supported him. It would be two years, full of draining physical therapies, before Cunningham managed to walk. But he never waivered in his determination.

Amazingly, he became a star runner. He was a college standout at the University of Kansas, and finished fourth in the 1500-meter race at both the 1932 and 1936 Olympics. In 1933 Cunningham received the James E Sullivan award as the most outstanding amateur athlete in the United States. The next year he set a new world record in the mile, 4:06.8.

Later in life Cunningham earned a PhD from New York University, and then returned to Kansas to open the Glenn Cunningham Youth Ranch. The ranch took care of nearly 10,000 needy and/or abused youth over a three-decade period.

In running and other pursuits, Cunningham often quoted his favorite Bible verse, Isaiah 30:41: "Those who wait on the Lord shall renew their strength; they shall mount up with wings like eagles, they shall run and not be weary, they shall walk and not faint."

CLARENCE DEMAR: Seven-time Boston winner and father of the aerobic revolution

Clarence DeMar won the 1911 Boston Marathon, and placed 12th in the next year's Stockholm Olympic Marathon. Then he stopped running. Why? He had many reasons.

First, doctors told him he had a potentially dangerous heart murmur. Second, DeMar was highly humble and religious. He felt it wrong to attract attention by winning races. Finally, he was taking courses at both Boston University and Harvard. Who had time for frivolous activities like running?

So DeMar stopped. When World War 1 loomed, he was drafted into the Army. He didn't return to running until 1922 when he set a Boston Marathon record, 2:18:10 (the course was about 24.5 miles). He then three-peated by winning the next two Bostons, and also won in 1927, 1928, and 1930 (at age 41).

That gave DeMar the still-standing record for total Boston Marathon victories: seven. He achieved this despite no wins during his prime from age 23 to age 34--the years when a temporary retirement and a World War put him on the sidelines.

DeMar contributed to running history even in his death from cancer at age 70 in 1958. His body was autopsied, and the results published by the New England Journal of Medicine. The primary finding: While his heart arteries had some blockage, they were so much wider than most, from all his endurance training, that there was plenty of room for healthy blood flow. This medical conclusion helped launch the aerobic fitness revolution.

BUDDY EDELEN: From "Butterball" to America's top marathon runner

Buddy Edelen had no future in distance running. As a child growing up in Kentucky, he was so fat that kids on the block called him "Butterball Buddy." He turned to running at the University of Minnesota, where he won the occasional 2-mile. But nothing impressive. No one knew his name.

In 1960, after college, Edelen moved to England, where road runners and marathoners seemed faster than in the U.S. He lived in a tiny apartment, taught school for the smallest of paychecks, and trained as never before. Previously, he had never run more than 6 or 7 miles at time. "Now I knock out 100 miles a week," he told one interviewer.

The more Edelen ran, the faster he got. In December, 1962, he ran a 2:18:57 marathon. Six months later, he set a world record, 2:14:28, to become the first runner under 2:15. Now he was a threat to make the 1964 U.S. Olympic Team.

He flew to Yonkers, New York, to encounter terrible, non-British weather: high-humidity and temps in the high 90s. No problem. He won the Olympic Marathon Trials by almost 20 minutes.

Four months later, at the Tokyo Olympics, Edelen finished a strong sixth, despite sciatic pain. Now he was both an Olympian and a world record holder in the marathon. His name was known in California, New England, and far more distant parts.

ROBERTA "BOBBI" GIBB: First woman (1966) to run the Boston Marathon

From her earliest years in the mid-1940s, Roberta "Bobbi" Gibb felt an almost mystical connection to all parts of the universe: the stars, the grains of sand on the beach, the woods near her home just outside Boston. They nourished her soul, and made her feel like running. So she did.

In her early 20s, she watched the Boston Marathon. Something grabbed her. "I felt I had discovered an ancient, lost, and yet civilized tribe of runners," she remembers. "They were in sync with the most primitive and natural human instincts. I decided I was going to run the Boston Marathon someday myself." Several years later, bolstered by training runs up to 40 miles, she wanted to join them. But race organizers turned down her entry, stating, "Women can't run the marathon. It's too long for them."

The next year, 1966, she simply showed up in Hopkinton, and jumped out from behind forsythia bushes to join the 500 men runners. She worried they might lash out at her. Instead they supported her. Typical remark? "Atta girl, you can do it. This is a public road and we'll take care of you." Gibb ran strong and smooth to the end, finishing in 3:20 to become Boston's first woman runner.

"I just wanted to question a repressive structure that prevented women from reaching their goals," she said. "People said women were not capable. But how do you know if you don't give them a chance in the first place?"

MIKI GORMAN: Short of stature, but big in toughness and marathon endurance

It's good to be young, a bit lean and long, and accomplished in other sports. But Miki Gorman violated all the rules: She was 33 when she started running in 1969, and stood not an inch over five feet tall. She weighed 88 pounds, none of it muscle.

Gorman, born in Japan but living in Los Angeles, stuck to her running anyway. "Once I decide to do something, I give it my absolute best," she said. After several years of running only in her gym, she discovered outdoor running, and won her first race. "That's when I realized that being small didn't have to hold me back," she said. "I gained a lot of confidence."

So much, in fact, that she entered a marathon in December, 1973. Incredibly, she won again, and set a new world record for women, 2:46:37. She was the shortest runner in the women's field, the oldest (38), and the fastest woman ever to run 26.2 miles.

From there, the diminutive Gorman was practically unstoppable. In 1974, she set a new course record in the Boston Marathon. Ten months later, in January, 1975, she gave birth to a daughter, Danielle. A year later, she won the New York City Marathon. In 1977, she won both Boston and New York, where, at age 41, she lowered her best time to 2:39:11.

"I wasn't timid anymore," she said. "I stayed a humble person, but I was proud that I worked very hard for what I achieved."

BOBBY HALL: First wheelchair racer and Boston Marathon champ

In many ways, Bobby Hall had a model childhood. Always smiling, enthusiastic, and energetic, he had plenty of friends. But one thing set him apart: He was in a wheelchair, due to childhood polio, and couldn't do sports.

In the early 1970s, Hall began to notice the marathon success of runners from around his home in Boston. He decided to steer his heavy, everyday wheelchair out onto the roads. "I didn't know how long a marathon was, and that didn't matter," he recalls. "It was just a challenge, and one I gladly accepted. You can't always take baby steps. Sometimes you need giant leaps."

In 1975, Hall wheeled his clunky chair the full 26.2 miles from Hopkinton to the Boston Marathon finish line, crossing it in 2:58. He didn't wear an official race number, however, or receive any award. Like the women runners a decade earlier, Hall was a Boston Marathon finisher without any status. That sucked.

He refused to give up, and kept knocking on the door. Hall argued that the Boston Marathon could establish an official wheelchair division that would provide opportunity and encouragement to challenged athletes. Two years later, he and several other "wheelers" were allowed as official entries.

Hall won, and improved his time to 2:40:40. "That's what it's all about--going faster and winning. Bill Rodgers said 'After Boston, there's only Heaven.' I agree. It stays with you forever."

JOANNA HARPER: Run like a boy. Run like a girl. Pioneer transgender scientist

Joanna Harper is one of the world's most influential, little-known runners who has done just that. She was a former low 2:20s male marathoner, who transitioned to female in 2004/5, and has continued training and racing hard as a woman. Her personal best times for the marathon, 2:23:55, in the Philadelphia Marathon in 1982, and winning the now-defunct Hamilton Marathon in 1981 were as a male.

Harper went out for the cross-country team as a high school freshman (male) in September 1971 and has run at least one race every calendar year since, making 48 consecutive years of racing. From 1971 through 2004 she competed in the men's category. Since 2005 she has competed in the women's category, starting hormone therapy in August 2004.

Within nine months she was running 12 percent slower but once she started racing in the women's category her age graded performances lined very well with her previous performances in the men's category (approximately 80 percent in either case).

Now as "an old lady" at 62, she has won team and individual USATF age group national championships. She has also studied what she has lived, becoming an Olympic consultant on transgender issues.In September 2019 Harper moved to England to work on a Ph.D. in exercise physiology.

JULIA HAWKINS: At 103, she's still going for gold in national championships

Not many people living today can recall attending a parade for the returning soldiers from World War I, but Julia Hawkins can. She can also run pretty fast for a 103-year–old. At the 2019 National Senior Games the sassy sprinter won gold in the 100-meter dash with a time of 46.07 seconds.

Born in 1916, she was raised in Louisiana and attended Louisiana State University. She managed to be a good student while working all kinds of jobs to help offset the cost of college. She waited on tables, was a messenger girl for a shoe store, and modeled. Her work ethic was boundless, a trait she would carry with her throughout life and on to masters competitions.

She was a fixture at the National Senior Games starting in 1995 and accrued three gold medals in the 5K and 10K time trials in cycling at age 80. She quit competing when there were no more competitors and decided to run instead.

She is the oldest woman to compete on an American track. She maintains her fitness by hauling around a 5-pound hose to water her Bonsai trees. "I'm always doing yard work and running for the phone," she explains. "This is how I stay in shape." Her advice on how to live a long healthy life is to keep busy and keep moving.

GEORGE HIRSCH: Publisher and leader, running strong in his mid-80s

At 75, most marathoners have hung up their shoes or are happy running in the back of pack just to finish. Not George Hirsch. He ran back-to-back marathons in times runners half his age would be proud of. His final two marathons in 2009 were just a few weeks apart, Chicago (3:58:39) and New York (4:06:14).

New York was the toughest. He didn't have a lot of recovery time and the course is harder. What he did have was the support of his longtime running buddies, Bill Rodgers, Amby Burfoot and German Silva who met him along the difficult parts of the course. At times he thought he might collapse but he dug deep and finished. Then found his wife and went out for cheesecake and coffee.

Hirsch had a long and distinguished career in magazine publishing, most notably as the founder of New York Magazine and a former publisher of Runner's World. He is currently the chairman of New York Road Runners.

Now 85, Hirsch can still run a 10:30-minute pace and afterwards do a Fun Run with his grandkids. He has lived a life centered on people, passion, principle, and running. Looking back on his 68 years of running, Hirsch feels blessed to have the stamina and passion to still run about four days a week and enter the occasional race in Central Park. He's had all the usual runner injuries but bounces back because that's what runners do. "Life is about comebacks," he likes to say.

SID HOWARD: Class clown to world class runner

Sid Howard has been featured in Runner's World and numerous other magazines for his world records. With his inviting smile and infectious personality, Sid looks like he has the world on a string. But it wasn't always so. In high school, Sid was an underachiever, the class clown. He was also the star runner.

But when he failed two subjects, he was thrown off the team, quit school, got married, had a child and joined the air force. Beating the odds, he stayed married and had five more kids, worked hard, started his own business and graduated college on the same day as his grandson.

When he was 39, his son told him there was a race in town for old men like him. Howard decided to show his kids that this old dude might still have it and won the 5K, sparking a drive to return to running. He ran the 1978 New York City Marathon with only three months of training. He flew for 20 miles, hit the wall at 22 dazed, disoriented, and starving. He begged for food from the spectators, which revived him enough to finish in 3:02.

That was the start of Howard's illustrious running career. He has won five world championships, 50 national championships, five world records and eight gold world champion medals. He also holds the American indoor 65-69 records of 2:19.4 for the 800, 5:23.05 for the mile, and 4:45.36 for 1500 meters.

At 80, Howard is still running and coaching. As he states, "My last race will finish at the casket. I'm going to jump in, close the lid, and feel like I lived a full life."

DICK HOYT: The man pushing disabled Rick Hoyt, and a father unlike any other

In his mid-30s, Dick Hoyt described himself as a "porker." He ate too much and exercised too little. But life was stretched thin, given all the care that his son Rick needed. Rick barely survived childbirth, his mother's umbilical cord wrapped around his head, nearly suffocating him. Doctors thought he would live in a "vegetative state."

Wrong. Eventually Rick went to public school, and graduated from college, using a computer-assisted wheelchair to type out words one slow letter at a time. At 15, he told his father, Dick, that he wanted to enter a 5-mile road race to raise funds for a classmate. Somehow, Dick got himself into shape and pushed his son the whole way. That night, Rick banged out a short message: "Dad, when we were running, I felt like I wasn't disabled anymore."

That did it! Dick Hoyt trained hard enough to become a marathoner, even an Ironman triathlete. And every time he ran 26.2 miles or swam-biked-and-ran a 15-hour Ironman Triathlon, he took Rick along with him. They became among the most famous and admired of all endurance athletes. There's even a statue honoring them in Hopkinton, MA, where the Boston Marathon starts.

Rick isn't a talker, but he understands the effort and love his father has bestowed on him. "No question, he's the father of the century," Rick types on his computer. "If there were one thing I could do in life, I'd put my father in a chair and push him through a race."

MEB KEFLEZIGHI: He won the most important marathon ever--Boston 2014

Meb Keflezighi was born in Eritrea, moved to the United States speaking no English, and won the most important marathon ever run--the 2014 Boston Marathon. His story, example, and words have inspired all who have heard them.

One of 10 children, Keflezighi began running in junior high, attended college at UCLA, and became a U.S. citizen in 1998. In the next decade, he set an American record for 10,000 meters, won the silver medal in the 2004 Olympic Marathon, and won the 2009 New York City Marathon.

Keflezighi did not run the 2013 Boston Marathon, where two finish-line bombs caused massive casualties, but was in a nearby hotel. He vowed to enter the next year. Like all other runners he wanted to reclaim the streets of Boston for the marathon participants and the spectators who gathered to support them.

Before the 2014 race, he wrote the names of those killed in 2013 on his bib. Keflezighi ranked only 15th among the superfast runners in the field, but made a bold move to the front midway. It seemed impossible that he could stay out front to the end, yet somehow he did. Just a month from 39, he kept repeating to himself: "Boston strong! Meb strong! Boston strong! Meb strong!" And then he snapped through the finish-line tape, the first American male to win Boston in more than 30 years.

Afterwards, he said he was inspired by thinking about the previous year's victims. "They helped carry me through," he noted.

"OLD JOHN" A. KELLEY: Two-time Boston champ and the first great masters runner

John Adelbert Kelley didn't appear to have a future in marathon running. He attempted the Boston Marathon as a 20-year-old in 1928, but couldn't go the distance. He failed again four years later. Zero for two. Maybe he should switch to bowling?

But instead, Kelley started Boston once more in 1933, and this time he got it right. He finished in 3:03:56. Two years later, he won Boston. In 1945, he won for the second time. In 1992, he finished Boston for the 58th time--a record that will be broken ... but not easily.

Kelley also ran in two Olympic Marathons on Team USA. In an era that predated age-group and "masters" running, he was a pioneering veteran runner who kept on ticking. To this day, no one has beat his record of 17 Boston Marathon finishes in 2:40 or under. In its special January 2000 issue, Runner's World magazine named Kelley "The Runner of the Century." No one argued with the choice.

In his later years, the song-loving Irishman would delight runners with his rendition of "Young at Heart." The words fit his life and his philosophy: "And if you should survive to a hundred and five / Look at all you'll derive out of bein' alive / And here is the best part, you have a head start / If you are among the very young at heart." There was rarely a dry eye in the room.

"YOUNG JOHN" J. KELLEY: Anxiety-prone Olympian and Boston winner

Stories of John Joseph Kelley or "Kel" are plentiful from stopping his car to assist a turtle crossing the street to losing the Boston Marathon because he wouldn't kick a dog out of his way. He was quiet but had tremendous drive. He also carried the weight of breaking America's losing streak at Boston.

Leading up to the 1957 Boston Marathon, the press hounded him from his home in Mystic CT to the school where he taught. Boston Race Director Jock Semple called him America's Only Hope to win Boston. He spent the night before the race at the home of John A. Kelley, his mentor. He couldn't eat or sleep and was plagued with thoughts of failure, his Irish demeanor sinking him into depression.

But Kelley was also a fierce fighter and his will to win stayed steadfast. By race day morning he had overcome his doubts and fears to become the first and only member of the BAA running club to win the Boston Marathon, the first American to win in 11 years and he set a new course record. Interestingly, the American drought after Kelley went on for 11 years till it was broken by Amby Burfoot, a protégé of Kelley's.

Kelley finished second at Boston five times, won the 1959 Pan American Games Marathon, captured eight consecutive USA National Marathon titles, and represented the United States in two Olympics. He is remembered for his kindness, his playful rebellious streak, playing Bob Dylan non-stop and being able to recount every marathon he ran. He was an American original.

STYLIANOS KYRIAKIDES: He won Boston for seven million starving Greeks

No one expected the starved and ragged Greek to win the 1946 Boston Marathon. But fueled by devotion to his countrymen, Stylianos Kyriakides came from war-ravaged Greece to raise funds and awareness about the plight of the post-WWII Greek people to win Boston in 2:29:27.

This was not his first Boston Marathon. He had met John A. Kelley at the 1936 Berlin Olympics and was invited by him to run the 1938 Boston Marathon. Kyriakides had to drop out of the marathon due to blisters from wearing new shoes. He vowed to come back and win it. But then WWII arrived. Greeks starved to death at astonishing rates. He bore the burden to win the marathon to help his people.

Seeing his malnourished fatigued frame upon arrival in Boston, doctors urged him to quit saying he would die in the streets. He hadn't trained or run distance in six years but he was ready to win or die. The favorite to win that year was Johnnie Kelley. They ran the last few miles stride for stride till Kyriakides pulled away to win. Following the race, Kyriakides stayed in the United States to raise funds and awareness for the Greek people.

When Kyriakides returned to Greece on he arrived with 25,000 tons of supplies in American aid — including $250,000 in cash. Approximately one million Greeks greeted him as a hero and the Athens Acropolis was illuminated in his honor. There is a sculpture of Kyriakides at the 1-mile mark of the Boston course. He is called the Miracle Marathoner.

LOPEZ LOMONG: A former "Lost Boy" finds new life in his new land

When 16-year-old Lopez Lomong got off his flight from Kenya to New York City, he expected to walk to his new home. After all, he had walked to the airport in Kenya, and walked and run his whole life before that as a "Lost Boy" of the Sudan. He was stunned to learn his new parents owned a car.

Taking his first shower, he nearly froze to death. So much cold water! He didn't realize a wall lever could make it warm, even hot. "I was shivering so hard," he remembers. "I thought that's how white people got white--with their cold showers."

At high school in Tully, New York, 20 miles south of Syracuse, Lomong joined the track team, excelling at the middle distances. He won three New York state titles, then attended Northern Arizona University. In 2007, he became a U.S. citizen, and in 2008, he made the U.S. Olympic that traveled to Beijing, China, to represent his new country.

His Olympic teammates considered Lomong so emblematic of the American dream that they elected him team captain. This meant that he was the first U.S. athlete to enter the Olympic Stadium during the Opening Ceremonies, and that he did so while carrying the U.S. flag.

"Before, I ran from danger and death," Lomong says. "Now I run for sport and to represent the country that saved me and showed me the way."

MATTHEW LONG: A 20-ton bus couldn't pin him down

On December 22, 2005, firefighter Matt Long was riding his bike to the New York City Fire Department training center when he was hit by a 20-ton bus and dragged under it. By the time emergency medical help arrived, he had a one percent chance of survival.

Long was put in a medically induced coma, remained in the hospital for five months, and required additional surgeries throughout the next two years. A feisty son of Brooklyn who enjoyed parties and kicking back at Irish bars in the neighborhood, Long's will to live and top physical condition helped him survive.

A titanium rod was placed through his left leg from his hip to his ankle. Metal screws kept the bones of his left foot in place. His right abductors were basically dead. He underwent several surgeries to heal his battered abdominal-wall muscles. His doctor warned that it could take two years before he could dispense with crutches or a cane.

After leaving the hospital Long fell into depression, holed up in his apartment thinking of what used to be. "It hurt to watch everyone around me continue with their lives," he stated. He decided to get back his life by running a marathon. He enlisted two buddies from the firehouse who were marathoners and trained through pain and self-doubts.

In 2008, with his doctors and fellow firefighters at his side, he ran the New York City Marathon in 7:21:22. Long is now married with three kids and opened a fitness gym in Danbury CT. He is proof that the sheer will to survive will trump a 20-ton bus.

ANNE MAHLUM: Running and organizing for the homeless

When you pass homeless people on the streets where you run, do avoid them? Keep your eyes down? Anne Mahlum decided to help them. Every morning, when 26-year-old Anne Mahlum started out on her daily run in Philadelphia she passed a group of homeless men at a shelter. One day she decided to wave to them. A few days later the men responded with sarcastic hellos of their own and a rapport began.

She started to think that running might be the ticket to help them get back on their feet. Mahlum met with the director of the shelter and asked if she could invite the men to join her on her runs. He agreed, and with a group of nine who were trying to improve their lives, she formed the seeds that would become Back on my Feet (BoMF), a national for-purpose 501c3 organization that uses running to help the homeless make changes in their lives that can lead to employment and independent living.

This is how BoMF works: interested members commit to run three times a week for 30 days. If they reach 90 percent attendance, they receive financial literacy classes and job skills training through corporate partners with the goal of gaining financial assistance. Back on My Feet alumnus have a success rate of 90% of members maintaining their employment.

Mahlum has won numerous awards and recognition for her work with the homeless. And runners who volunteer to run with BoMF say it has changed their lives and given them more understanding and respect for people in shelters. What started with a wave, turned into a tsunami of goodwill.

TATYANA MCFADDEN: From a Russian orphanage to a multi-marathon winner

Born with Spina Bifida and left in a Russian orphanage, Tatyana McFadden was adopted at the age of six by Debbie McFadden and brought to the US. She started wheelchair racing in high school and by age 15 became the youngest member of the 2004 Paralympics team.

She taught herself how to walk by using her arms as legs to get around the orphanage. After being brought to the US and getting fitted for a wheelchair, she raced her purple chair up and down the dead-end street where she lived in Maryland, acting like any other adolescent. She was raised to believe she could do anything.

At the 2012 London Paralympics she won three gold medals. In 2013 she won the Boston, London, Chicago and New York marathons, becoming the first man or woman, able-bodied or disabled, to win the Grand Slam (four World Major Marathons in the same year) and then repeated her Grand Slam victory in 2014, 2015 and 2016.

McFadden helped write the Americans With Disabilities Act of 1990, the milestone legislation that prohibits discrimination based on disability. Her portrait is at the National Portrait Gallery in Washington D.C. The Russian phrase "Ya sama!" can be translated as "I can do it." She learned it as a young child in her St. Petersburg orphanage and uses it now when faced with a challenge. She makes the impossible happen.

DAVE MCGILLIVRAY: Indestructible until the day he needed triple-bypass surgery

Growing up, Dave McGillivray developed an inferiority complex. He was shorter than his peers, and not quickly picked for any sports teams. In fact, he titled his autobiography "Last Chosen." Short, yes, but few have ever brought more focus and determination to their efforts.

McGillivray graduated as the high school valedictorian in 1972, and six years later ran from Medford, OR, to his hometown,  Medford, MA, averaging 42 miles a day. Along the way he raised funds for the Jimmy Fund, and finished to great acclaim inside Fenway Park.

Endurance became McGillivray's hallmark. In 1980, he completed his first Ironman Triathlon. And he ran the Boston Marathon every year. Ten in a row. Twenty in a row. After he became Boston's race director in 2001, he continued running from Hopkinton to Boston in the post-race darkness. Thirty in a row. Forty in a row. In 2018 he even ran seven marathons in seven days on seven continents. He seemed unstoppable.

Not quite. In a shock to himself and many others, McGillivray learned in 2018 that he needed triple-bypass surgery. He got the surgery, and followed his doctor's orders: no running for two months. Then he slowly started building up to his 2019 Boston run. On Patriots Day, at age 64, he finished his 47th Boston in a row. It was slower than his others. And more meaningful. "That was my toughest and most challenging marathon ever," he admitted. "But it was also the most special."

CHARLES MILLIMAN: Celebrating an 85th birthday with 85 miles

Chuck Milliman is not your average octogenarian. On his 80th birthday he ran 80 miles. That was so much fun he ran 85 miles on his 85th birthday. When he's not running, he is practicing the pole vault in his backyard pit that he built with his son. This retired pastor knows how to live a fulfilled life. With Shirley, his wife of 68 years by his side there doesn't seem to be much that Milliman can't do.

Milliman grew up in Hooper, Washington during the Depression. Their home had no electricity or running water. "Going to the outhouse in zero degrees was tough," says Milliman. He ran his first marathon at 40, crying like a baby the whole way, swearing he'd never do that again. He now holds a 25-year streak at that marathon.

For his 85-miler, he struggled to keep his mental side alert, especially during the cold rainy nights. "At times I thought I would lose my mind out there," recalls Milliman. "I did the multiplication tables, worked on my pace, whatever it took to keep alert and not think about the pain." Bolstered by his son-in-law and a friend, they both grabbed an arm and supported him through the last 4 miles, finishing in 34 hours and 35 minutes.

At 86, he laughs off suggestions that he should quit. "I'm still out there and feel great," he laughs. "As long as my body can stay up-right I'll compete. I run for the sheer enjoyment of being able to run. And I thank God every day for my health and that I can still run."

BILLY MILLS: Biggest upset winner in Olympic distance-running history

Billy Mills was born into South Dakota's Ogala Lakota Indian tribe in 1938. His family gave him the name "Tamakoce Te'Hila," which means "loves his country" or "respects the earth." Orphaned at 12, Mills took up boxing and running a few years later at a Kansas high school for Indian youth. "I was constantly told and challenged to live my life as a warrior," he said. "As a warrior you assume responsibility for yourself."

At the University of Kansas, Mills began to excel at cross-country running. After graduating, he joined the U.S. Marines, and finished second in the 10,000-meter race at the U.S. Olympic Track Trials in 1964. That gained him a trip to the Tokyo Olympics, where he was considered an also-ran among the world's best.

Mills ran the first 5000 meters in Tokyo just a couple of seconds slower than his personal best. He still had 5000 meters to go, and it seemed impossible that he could stay with the leaders. But somehow he did. He hung on, hung on, and hung on, following the big favorite, Ron Clarke, from Australia.

With one-half lap remaining in the 25-lap race, Mills found the power to rocket to the front. Clarke and others gave chase but to no avail. Mills's victory is considered one of the greatest Olympic upsets ever. "Coming off the last turn," he says, "my thoughts changed from 'one more lap, one more lap' to 'I can win! I can win! I can win!'"

GARY MUHRCKE: Winner of the first New York City Marathon in 1970

Fighting fires all night didn't douse the spirit or speed of Gary Muhrcke, winner of the first New York City Marathon in 1970, with a course of four laps around Central Park. The 30-year-old New York City fireman hadn't trained much due to an injury and was sleep deprived after battling blazes all night but he was a marathoner and that's what marathoners do. They show up.

He drove in from his home in Long Island with his wife, Jane, their three kids, and paid his $1.00 entry fee. The 85-degree heat didn't slow him down and he won in 2:31:39. For his effort, he won a trophy and a watch. The trophy is now broken and the watch wore out.

Winning the first New York City Marathon was not a big deal to Muhrcke, a two-time winner of the Yonkers Marathon. The next day at the firehouse it wasn't even mentioned. "I was just a strange person who ran," he recalls. "No one was interested in runners back then."

With his wife Jane, they opened the chain of Super Runner stores. He recently sold them but held on to the original store and operates it with his daughter. Jane still makes, by hand, the laurel wreaths that adorn the heads of the winners at the New York City Marathon.

AMY PALMIERO-WINTERS: A leg amputation didn't stop her from ultrarunning

Most able-bodied runners wouldn't think of running the Marathon des Sables, a race of 140 miles in six days through the Sahara Desert, with an average temperature of 122. But that's what Amy-Palmiero-Winters did in April of 2019 becoming the first female amputee to complete the grueling race. Her 13-year-old daughter gave her a note that was laminated and hung from her rucksack: "Good luck. I love you. Don't die."

Palmiero-Winters, a single mom of two teenage kids from Hicksville, NY, had her left leg amputated below the knee following a motorcycle accident in 1997. A former track and cross-country runner in high school with the dream of becoming an Olympian, she was even more determined to push through the obstacles and become the elite athlete she still dreamed of becoming.

Palmiero-Winters never gives less than 100 percent in anything she does and that determination has paid off. She holds eleven world records in various events and is the first female amputee to finish the Badwater Ultramarathon, a 135-mile race from Death Valley to the Mount Whitney trailhead. To prepare her body for the desert heat she did burpees and lunges in a sauna.

Why does she do such extreme events? "I want my children to understand about pushing the envelope and not selling themselves short," she states. "Push past what you think you are capable of and you'll surprise yourself."

JAMIE PARKS: A long (rewarding) wait for love

What would you do for love? Wait seven years to marry the woman you loved who lay in a coma? Give up running (solo) marathons to push her in a wheelchair so she didn't have to wait alone at the finish? Jamie Parks did all that and more for Lynn, the woman he loves.

Five months before their wedding, Lynn was involved in a car crash and suffered a brainstem injury and was not expected to live. She was in a coma for seventeen days. Jamie was told to prepare for the worst, but Lynn pushed through. When she was able to speak, she told Jamie she would marry him when she could walk down the aisle.

Seven years later Lynn walked down the aisle to exchange their wedding vows. An avid runner, Jamie took Lynn to his races, leaving her at the start in a wheelchair but he always felt badly. Inspired by Dick and Richard Holt, a father and son team that run the Boston Marathon with Dick pushing his son who has cerebral palsy, Jamie started pushing her in races in 1991. To date they've covered more than 27,500 miles together.

Their personal bests include a 17:35 5K and 2:57 at the 1996 Chicago Marathon. Pretty amazing times considering the weight Jamie pushes (Lynn and the chair combined weigh 170 pounds).

They compete in Jamie's age category, not the wheelchair division, and have won several races outright. Their story was filmed for a documentary featuring Lynn and Jamie called Marathon Love, which has won several film-festival awards. In 2002, they carried the Olympic torch through Chicago on its way to the Winter Olympics in Salt Lake City, Utah. Now that's love!

SARAH REINERTSEN: Seven marathons, seven continents, seven days, one leg

Running seven marathons on seven continents in seven days is just another run-of-the-mill challenge for Sarah Reinertsen, an above-the-knee Paralympian. The five-foot tall stack of dynamite leaves nothing on the table when she decides to take on a quest.

At age seven, Reinertsen had her leg amputated due to a birth defect. Determined to be the athlete she knew she was, at her first international track meet at 13, she broke the 100m-world record for female above-knee amputees and went on to break it record several times.

Walking is a challenge, as her gait requires a different swing pattern, a combination of lifting and swinging the hip to make the hinges of the prosthesis articulate in a way that mimics a natural gait. Try that while running marathons.

The one title that eluded her at the first attempt was being the first female ATK amputee to complete the World Championship Ironman in 2004. Crushed, she told everyone, "I'll be back next year. I've got unfinished business." She trained even harder. In 2005 she crossed the Ironman finish line with two hours to spare before the cutoff.

Reinertsen has been featured in Nike ads, is the recipient of the ESPY Award for best Female Disabled Athlete of the Year, and the inspiration for the Nike "Sarah sole" first ever running shoe for a prosthetic. She mentors other disabled athletes, especially kids, by teaching them how to run, spin, bike and swim. Reinertsen is living life to the fullest.

BILL RODGERS: Smoker-motorcyclist to Boston Billy, King of the Roads

Bill Rodgers wasn't always known as "Boston Billy." Prior to his marathon career, he was a heavy smoker in a dead-end (literally) job, wheeling bodies to the morgue at a Boston hospital. After running cross-country at Wesleyan University with teammates Amby Burfoot and Jeff Galloway, Bill Rodgers had quit running when he graduated in 1970.

He didn't understand Burfoot's and Galloway's dedication to getting up early for 20-milers on weekend mornings. Staying out late and having fun was more his thing. Rodgers started smoking and was aimless, a former runner without a cause. As he watched the 1971 Boston Marathon and saw his former teammates Burfoot and Galloway out front, he had a thought that changed his life: "I can do that!"

Rodgers quit smoking and got back in shape. But he underestimated the marathon and dropped out of his first Boston attempt in 1973. That's when he understood he'd have to train smarter and harder. He won Boston in 1975, and ended his career with four Boston wins, four New York City wins, and 14 other major marathons.

At 60, Rodgers was diagnosed with prostate cancer, and underwent a radical prostatectomy in 2008. He has made it his mission to share his experience and promote awareness of the disease. He's still running and racing, and remains a popular, engaging speaker at many annual events, talking about his career, his books, and his many running buddies. Just don't ask for nutrition tips; he has been known to eat mayonnaise straight from the jar.

ED ROUSSEAU: He stopped drinking, started running, and finished 109 marathons

Nothing could stop Ed Rousseau from his drinking. Not a divorce or countless DUIs. Then he discovered marathons and now fuels his addiction with miles instead of alcohol. At 80 he has run 109 marathons (some on snowshoes) and 121 ultras. He loves races with "hours" in the title as in 72-hour races, and then there are the "day" races, as in the six-day race he ran totaling 384 miles. "It's either run or head for a recliner," says Rousseau. What he is most proud of, despite his numerous age-group records, is his 36 years of sobriety.

At 17, he enlisted in the air force. He had to run three miles on a track and realized he had a talent for running. He also started drinking. Alcoholism runs in his family and he became its next victim.

After the Air Force he worked for a data corporation and was sent to Tehran. Right before the 1978 coup, the Iranian military issued a nighttime curfew of 9:00pm or risk getting shot. At 8:45, Rousseau sprinted the mile back from his buddy's apartment where they met to drink, just avoiding the bullets. Returning to the states, he entered AA but fell off the wagon.

During his second stint at sobriety, he ran every day. He signed up for the inaugural Twin Cities Marathon in 1982 and is now one of only 23 left of the charter members, and the oldest one. Running saved his life and provided him with a group of people who are like family to him. He volunteers at AA meetings and other treatment centers as a motivational speaker. "If I don't give back, I may fall back," he reminds himself. He has been inducted into the Minnesota Running Legends and the Michigan Upper Peninsula Road Runners Hall of Fame.

WILMA RUDOLPH: From sickly child to Olympic gold-medal sprint sensation

Stricken at birth with double pneumonia, polio and scarlett fever didn't prevent Wilma Rudolph from becoming the first American woman to win three gold medals in track and field at the 1960 Olympics in Rome. Born prematurely in 1940, the 20th of 22 siblings, she was disabled for most of her childhood due to infantile paralysis. She wore a leg brace until she was 12.

A naturally gifted runner, while still in high school she was recruited to train with Tennessee State University at age 16 and qualified in the 200-meter for the 1956 U.S. Olympic team. Although defeated in the 200-meter, she and her team of Tigerbelles won the bronze in the 4x100m relay with Rudolph running the third leg. While a sophomore at TSU, she qualified for the 1960 Olympics in Rome and won three gold medals; the 100 and 200 - meter sprints and the 4x100 meter relay.

When she returned to Tennessee, she was welcomed with a parade that she insisted become integrated. Rudolph became the most highly visible African-American woman around the world.

After retiring from competition, she went on to teach, coach and run a community center. In 1994 she was diagnosed with brain cancer and died five months later at the age of 54. She was inducted into several sports halls of fame and lauded as one of the five greatest female athletes in the United States. TSU named their indoor track in her memory. In 2004, the United States Postal Service featured her on a 23-cent stamp.

JIM RYUN: A Kansas high-schooler finds his sport, and breaks impossible barriers

Like many awkward teens, Jim Ryun was desperate to find a sport. But he seemed too gangly and uncoordinated for any. "I was cut from the church baseball team," he remembers. "I was cut from the junior-high baseball team. I'd go to bed at night and pray, 'Dear God: If you've got a plan for my life, please show up sooner rather than later, because things aren't going very well."

Happily, something did appear: He could run. And he was not afraid. At Wichita (KA) East high school, a coach told him, "To make progress, you've got to push back the pain barrier." Okay, not a problem.

Ryun pushed back harder than anyone before him. As a sophomore, he ran the mile in 4:07.8. The next June, 1964, he traveled to a big time "open" meet in Compton, CA. It was full of world-famous milers from around the globe. Still, all eyes were glued on the high-school junior from Kansas.

He finished eighth, not very impressive, but the stopwatch was more important. It read an impossible 3:59. Ryun had made history; he was the first high-school miler to break 4 minutes in the mile. The next year, as a senior, he improved to 3:55.3--a record that lasted 36 years.

In 1967 Ryun lowered the mile world record to 3:51.1. At the 1968 Mexico City Olympics, he won the silver medal in the 1500 meters. Not bad for a klutzy kid from Kansas.

BRIAN SALZBERG: He has run every Falmouth Road Race ... even with a brain tumor

Streakers are a bunch of dedicated, tough dudes, some would say fanatical, who don't let anything get in the way of their streak. But what does a streaker do with a broken foot or when diagnosed with a brain tumor? If you're Brian Salzberg, who holds the streak record with four others at the Falmouth Road Race, you don't let little things like that stop you.

Salzberg ran his first Falmouth Road Race in 1973, and got hooked. "I can see in my mind Johnny Kelley who was 65 at the time spiffed up in a Hawaiian shirt jitterbugging with his wife," he recalls. "I loved it." That was the start of the streak.

But injures would follow. A few weeks after the 2003 road race, Salzberg was told he had a benign brain tumor and underwent surgery to remove it. Two weeks later, he began having problems related to the procedure and had to undergo another round of brain surgery. This time his docs said that he couldn't run for six months. But walking? Yeah, that would be okay. In 2004 he walked the 7-mile race in one hour and 45 minutes, keeping the streak alive.

In 2008, he damaged ligaments in his foot and completed the race on crutches. In 2010, the tumor returned and was told that he wouldn't be able to compete in the race as it was too soon after his surgery. So he walked the course. All in all, he's had nine surgeries, including the three for benign brain tumors), two back surgeries, and knee, hip, and hamstring operations. None of these injuries has prevented him from breaking his string of 47 (as of Aug 2019) successive Falmouth Road Races. Salzberg is one dedicated streaker.

GEORGE SHEEHAN: Runner, racer, medical doctor, and writer extraordinaire

George Sheehan didn't have a moment to spare. In his mid-40s, he already had 12 children, a busy cardiology practice, and a pile of great thinkers' books on his nightstand. He enjoyed philosophy as much as he did medical science.

One evening, perhaps remembering his track days in college, Sheehan took a spin around his backyard in Rumsford, New Jersey. He had staked out a course with 26 laps to the mile. Something lit a spark. Later he would write, "The true runner is a very fortunate person. He has found something in him that is just perfect."

Sheehan kept running and reading, and soon added writing to his regimen. At 50, he became the first person to run a sub-5-mile at his age. He challenged himself with longer distances like the Boston Marathon, which gave him more time for thinking on the run. In the early 1970s, he also began writing a popular column for Runner's World magazine.

The column and several best-selling books invited others to see a new side of running--introspective and highly personal. Sheehan always celebrated the individual. "If you don't have a challenge, find one," he wrote. And also: "Success means having the courage, the determination, and the will to become the person you were meant to be."

When Sheehan developed prostate cancer in his 60s, he searched for new truths. In his last interview, he explained that he had once entered races to compete against other runners. Now, however: "I've learned there is only one person in this race, and I am it."

KATHRINE SWITZER: She finished Boston despite being attacked by a race official

As a high schooler in the early 1960s, Kathrine Switzer wanted to be a cheerleader. But her father said, "You shouldn't be cheering for others. You should play a sport where they cheer for you." Switzer tried field hockey, but had no skills. She was only good at running up and down the field.

Five years later, in 1967, Switzer stood at the Boston Marathon start line with her coach, Arnie Briggs. She had spent the Syracuse, NY, winter training with Briggs, so he entered her with the name "K.V. Switzer." Boston organizers thought her a man, and gave her race number 261.

Several miles into the race, a Boston official named "Jock Semple" recognized the woman's body under Switzer's sweat suit. He jumped off the bus, snarling, to charge after Switzer, and remove her number. However, her hammer-thrower boyfriend body blocked Semple. "Run like hell," Briggs yelled to Switzer, and that's what the two did, all the way to the Boston finish line in 4:20.

The photos of Semple apparently attacking Switzer flashed around the world. Eventually, they helped her promote a women's marathon in the Olympics. The effort was successful, with Joan Benoit winning the inaugural event in 1984. "That race fulfilled all my dreams," Switzer says. "The Olympic Marathon showed the entire world how physical and powerful women could be."

Switzer later formed a nonprofit organization, "261 Fearless," to encourage more women to run. Best of all, she and Semple became lasting friends.

MARKELLE TAYLOR: He served 18 years in prison, then ran a great marathon

Not many runners become marathoners while in prison serving nearly 18 years for second-degree murder. Markelle Taylor, the Gazelle of San Quentin State Prison, ran his first four marathons behind bars.

As a child, he grew up in a violent and abusive household. He ran track in high school and started junior college but dropped out. By his 20s he was addicted to alcohol and had a history of violence. Taylor was 27 when he assaulted his pregnant girlfriend, which led to the eventual death of the unborn child and his sentencing. San Quentin is a role model for being a progressive prison. Taylor took acting lessons, was baptized in the prison chapel, and enrolled in programs for anger management and substance abuse. He became a model prisoner.

He started running on the San Quentin 1000 Mile Club, coached by accomplished runners in the Bay area. "Running helped me through my time and despair," says Taylor. "It was a form of freedom." One particular coach, Ruona, former president of the Tamalpa Runners in Marin County, took him under his wing and trained him to run marathons. He qualified for the 2019 Boston Marathon by running the San Quentin marathon, where he powered through 104½ quarter-mile loops around the prison's lower yard. At Boston, he finished in just over three hours and felt he could have run faster.

Taylor is currently on parole. He started a job and shares a room with three other men, his running clothes scattered around the floor. "Prison saved my life. It made me a better person. A life sentence forces you to wake up," he says.

OPRAH WINFREY: Simply the most-famous person ever to finish a marathon

Running your first marathon is never easy--so long a distance, so many unexpected obstacles en route. Oprah Winfrey faced these, and much more, when she entered the 1994 Marine Corps Marathon in Washington, D.C. From the moment she woke up in her hotel room, Oprah was dogged by photographers from the National Enquirer. They followed her down the hall, into her elevator, and out to the starting line next to the National Cemetery.

Winfred tried to hide under a thick, black hoodie. But it didn't fool the media or the other 25,000 runners. Many ran over to clap her on the shoulder. "You're my hero, Oprah--great to see you out here," they said. Or maybe: "Oprah, I watch your show every afternoon. Wouldn't miss it." She responded with a friendly glance and thank-you gesture.

For as long as she could. After 13 miles, Oprah had to turn inward. She stared down at the pavement, and focused on moving her legs: one-two, one-two. Oprah had been training for 18 months. She had lost 60 pounds. She wanted to achieve something momentous in this, the 40th year of her life.

And she did. On the final, torturous climb to the Iwo Jima Memorial, Winfrey actually increased her pace. She finished in 4:29, a powerful statement. Later she often spoke about her run. "Life is a lot like the marathon," she said. "If you can finish a marathon, you can do anything you want."

BART YASSO: After terrible Lyme Disease, he ran the 56-mile Comrades Marathon

Running the Comrades Marathon, 56 miles through South Africa, is brutal under any condition. But to run it with Lyme disease is extraordinary. And that's what Bart Yasso, the retired Chief Running Officer at Runner's World did in 2010 at age 55. He describes crossing the finish line and seeing the Comrades logo as sheer Nirvana. He finished in 11 hours and 33 minutes, plenty of time left before the gate dropped at the 12-hour time limit.

Yasso contracted Lyme in 1990. While the disease slowed him down it didn't always stop him from running. It paralyzed the right side of his body and face and caused damage to his right hip joints, ankle and knee. He doesn't get that smooth runner's stride and is in pain most of the time. But to Yasso, who has run races on all seven continents, completed Badwater (146 miles), six Ironmans and biked across the USA twice, it was just "one of those things that you have to deal with."

Yasso wasn't always a lean, mean running machine. In his early twenties he was aimless, leading a risky life of smoking, drinking, and other not so great stuff. Challenged by his older brother George to run a 10K, Yasso didn't train but George did and beat the pants off him. That's when Yasso turned into a runner. He ran 100-mile weeks at his peak.

Living with Lyme has its good stretches and bad. Yasso rides out the bad and does the best he can. He watches what he eats and makes sure to get a lot of sleep. It's a condition that doesn't go away and the best thing is to learn to live with it. And decide to finally run Comrades.

TIMELESS WISDOM

Running is not so much a science as it is a sport built on collected knowledge. Sure, we have BMI, vo2 max, glycogen storage, and slow-twitch muscle fibers. These are fascinating measures, but they teach us only fractional lessons.

If you really want to know the truth about some running question, go to other runners, and ask them. What shoes work the best for you? What gel gives a nice burst of energy without an upset stomach? What marathon is the best organized and has the most interesting course? Do you always crave ice cream after your long runs?

We have a good name for these veteran runners all around us: They are Roads Scholars. You don't need to ask if they have a "PhD" after their name. Just look for the wear on their running shoes, and the race t-shirts in their collection.

The advice contained on the following pages comes in part from us, and our collective 200,000 miles of running. But, even more, it comes from the thousands of friendly runners we have met and talked to through the years.

We are grateful for all they have shared, and hope you benefit from their wise counsel. Most important of all, pass it along.

TRAINING: The Talk Test

It's Okay, Even Smart, To Run Slow And Conversational

If you listen to a little runner conversation, it won't be long before you hear the term "talk test." This has nothing to do with vocabulary-building. And it's not really a test; it won't help you determine your IQ or whether your major subject in college should be math or art history.

The talk test is actually about your running pace. It's a great way to gauge your best, most efficient running pace without using a watch, heart-rate monitor, and any other device. Just chat with your running partner, or even an imaginary partner if you happen to be running alone.

If you can hold a simple conversation without huffing, puffing, and gasping, then you have passed the talk test. You're running at a good and fitness-enhancing pace. If you can't get out more than one or two words at a time, slow down, you move too fast.

The Bottom Line: The "Talk Test" teaches one of the most important principles in running. You don't have to run fast and get out of breath. Indeed, you shouldn't. The goal is to find a relaxed, comfortable running pace. If you can talk normally, you've succeeded.

TRAINING: Recovery Days

Follow A Hard-Day/Easy-Day Pattern Of Training

Running is one of the most vigorous--if not the absolute most vigorous--off all forms of exercise. It pushes the heart hard, and also stresses the joints and muscles. That's the good news. That's why running is such a healthy activity.

It also means that too much running can push you over the edge. You will risk overtraining or an overuse injury. That's why famous coaches, especially the University of Oregon's legendary Bill Bowerman, long ago developed the hard-easy system of running. It means: Any day you run longer or faster than usual should be followed by a day of easy, relaxed, recovery running.

Or two. Especially if you are getting older, coming back from an injury or illness, or simply have too many other stresses in your life at the moment. The stress of hard training is essential to getting fitter, but too much stress has the opposite effect. It requires a delicate balance.

The Bottom Line: Pay attention to the effort required from each day of training. If one day is tough, make the next one--or several--much easier. Don't tip the scales too much in one direction.

TRAINING: Partners

Take Advantage. Training Partners Are The Best

Running is a wonderful solo activity. So simple and uncomplicated. You can squeeze a workout into any nick or cranny of your day without having to coordinate with a dozen others. No corporate meetings! Just lace up your shoes, open the door, and set out to greet the world. Ah, the rare tranquility.

However, social running is fantastic too. It's the best, most-enjoyable form of running motivation. A training partner provides some get-up-and-go when yours is lacking, a welcome listener when you need one, and a source of jokes, social commentary, and mindless banter to make the miles flow faster. He or she can help you through nasty weather, tough long runs, and lung-busting speed workouts.

In short, a training partner or partners makes every mile go easier. That's a good thing. Everyone needs it at some time, even if just once a week. Find one or several training partners. You'll be glad you did.

The Bottom Line: We believe that training partners are a runner's best friend. They rank right up there with a supportive spouse. Check with local running clubs, retail stores, or online social-media groups to locate nearby compatible runners.

TRAINING: More Miles

When Increasing Mileage, Follow "The 10 Percent Rule"

Nobody knows for sure where it came from. Women's Running book author Joan Ullyot, MD, thinks she might have invented it in the mid-1970s to break her own problem with recurrent injuries. At any rate, decades of runners have followed "The 10 Percent Rule" to make sure they don't get injured from doing too much, too soon, too fast.

Here's how it works. When things are going well, you need a way to plan next week's (and next month's) mileage. The 10 Percent Rule says that you can safely add 10 percent per week. A progression might look like this: 10 miles, 11 miles, 12 miles. Or 20 miles, 22 miles, 24 miles.

There will never be a way to guarantee that you don't get injured, but The 10 Percent Rule at least gives you a formula. Even better, it's a conservative one that has been working for runners for half a century.

The Bottom Line: Increase your weekly mileage by no more than 10 percent per week. To improve this formula, add an additional wrinkle: Every fourth week, decrease your training by 20 percent. Then, on week 5, do 10 percent more than week 3, and continue building.

TRAINING: Intervals

The Most Researched Way To Improve Your Race Pace

"Interval training" is the most long-standing and proven type of endurance training. It has been used by runners for nearly 100 years, and has been verified by hundreds of scientific papers.

Everyone from Olympians to back-of-the back runners can improve their race times through judicious use of interval training. It's the ultimate way to increase your cardiorespiratory fitness. Also, while arduous to do, interval training is easy to break down and understand.

The best interval workouts alternate 4 to 5 minutes of hard running with half that time of slow jogging or walking for recovery. For example, you might run 3 x 800 to 1200 meters hard with a 400-meter jog between the 800s. Pace is very important in interval workouts. You should aim to run the hard 4 to 5 minutes at your current 5K race pace or slightly faster. You can also do shorter repeats (100 meters to 400 meters) at a somewhat faster pace.

Bottom line: Run an interval workout once every week or two. But don't continue doing them for more than 8 weeks at a stretch. While intervals can give a big boost to your performance, they also lead to burnout and injury when overdone.

TRAINING: Tempo Runs

Run Hard But Controlled For Extra Strength-Endurance

Tempo runs are a relatively new addition to the runner's training tool kit. Before coach Jack Daniels's pioneering work in the 1990s, a few athletes did occasional long-steady efforts, but they didn't have a name, which meant they followed by few. Now, virtually all half marathoners and marathoners do tempo runs. They condition you to hard, fast, sustainable running without unnecessary fatigue.

The problem: Runners are often guilty of believing "more is better," and some have extended their tempo runs to 10 or 12 miles, or more. We think that's a potential mistake. They should last just 20 to 30 minutes.

The tempo run pace is often described as "hard but controlled." That's fine. If you want more precision, pick a pace a little faster than your half-marathon race pace. Sure, you could go faster, but resist the temptation. Tempo runs are supposed to make you stronger, not exhausted.

The Bottom Line: Once every week or every two weeks, run for 20-25 minutes a little faster than your half-marathon pace. You should finish the run feeling pleasantly fatigued, but not exhausted. To add more miles (and endurance) to your workout, do several miles of slow, relaxed running before and after your tempo run.

TRAINING: Long Runs

Do What You Need To Do. Keep The Pace Relaxed

All distance runners, even milers, should do a "long run" every week or two. There's no better way to build your strength, endurance, and running economy. On average, your long run should be 50- to 100-percent longer than the distance of your most-typical run.

If you normally cover about 4 miles, aim for 6 to 8 miles on your long-run day. If 30 minutes is typical, aim for 45 to 60 minutes. Keep the pace relaxed and comfortable; don't push it. Just extend the total time on your feet.

Marathoners need to pay special attention to long runs, since their race distance is so uniquely fatiguing. In America, marathoners try to cover 20 miles at a time; in Europe, 30 kilometers is more customary. Either will get the job done, as will 16 milers if that's all the time or fitness you have.

The Bottom Line: It has become popular to run hard over the final miles of a long run. We disagree with that approach. It might work, occasionally, for sub-3-hour marathoners, but not for most runners. Keep the pace easy on long runs to avoid injury. Do your faster running on another day that's geared to speedier paces.

TRAINING: Hills

Build Strength, Speed, And Stamina All At Once

We know no form of training that's better for distance runners than hill running. They add resistance work to your cardio, improve your efficiency, build speed, and have a relatively low risk for injury (at least the uphills; be cautious on downhills).

The Kenyan runners who win many of the world's biggest marathons are famous for their hill running in and around the Rift Valley. What else do you need to know?

The secret behind consistent hill running? No doubt, it's a combination of things. They build strength, because you are working against gravity. They stress the cardio system for the same reason. They teach good form; you're not likely to over stride on the hills. They build mental toughness; if you can run up steep hills, you can run anywhere. Hills make you run slower, with less pounding. The list goes on and on.

The Bottom line: Make hill running a regular part of your training program. Include hills on your long runs, and do fast, short hill repeats in your neighborhood or wherever you can find a challenging, smooth hill on a safe road or trail. Hills make you physically and mentally stronger.

TRAINING: Fartlek

Run Free, Run Natural, Run Strong

Originally, Swedish fartlek training took place on soft pine-needle trails in the deep woods. We wish it still did. Grass, parklands, and trails continue to make ideal places for an invigorating fartlek run. But you can do fartlek anywhere, and use if in training for any distance.

In a fartlek session, you run hard for a certain distance, then slow, then hard again. You don't use a watch; you run according to your feelings. You can go hard on hills, or walk the hills. You can run fast at sprint speed, or a bit slower (but still faster than normal) at half-marathon pace.

You jog (or walk) your recoveries until you feel like pushing the effort again. Take your time. You don't have to set off in 30 seconds or two minutes. There are no rules and no limits with fartlek training. There are no limits on fartlek training--only your willingness to experiment and be creative.

The Bottom Line: You can train hard without resorting to intervals, tempos, or any other tightly regulated workout. Try fartlek. Take off the reins. Run hard, recover until you feel refreshed, then go hard again.

TRAINING: HIT Workouts

Can You Achieve More With Less? Maybe

While interval training has been popular for 80 years, a form of super-intense intervals has gained recent attention. It's called HIT or HIIT training (High Intensity Training or High Intensity Interval Training). Proponents claim short, fast HIT intervals of 20 to 30 seconds can produce fitness gains as great as steady runs taking twice as long.

Is this possible? Yes, the physiological evidence is convincing. But don't get too excited about HIT workouts. For one thing, they are more likely to produce injuries. For another, distance races last far longer than 30 seconds, and other forms of training are crucial for successful 5Ks to marathons.

We do like the 30-20-10 workout that has been shown effective in several research reports. Run 30 seconds slow, 20 seconds moderate, and 10 seconds fast. Repeat a few times, recover with 10 minutes of slow running, and then start the 30-20-10s again. Intense, but also fun.

The Bottom Line: HIT intervals are super hard (but last only a short time), and can be super-effective. The keys: Build basic fitness first, and then do HIT workouts just once every week or two. They should make up a small percent of your training program.

TRAINING: Periodization

Build A Strong Base, Then Add More Varied Workouts

There are two similar definitions of "periodization" in training for runners. The first refers to building a solid mileage base before moving on to more intense training and eventually tapering to a peak. Many different workouts are part of the "mix," including easy runs, tempo runs, and interval speed work. This definition has been around for a long time, and the approach is both common-sense and proven effective.

The second, newer definition of periodization refers to the way you structure your workouts as you are reaching your major goal races. Here we're talking only about the last 3 to 8 weeks of your training block. In this kind of periodized training, you drop many of the tempo-type workouts, and end up running mainly easy days and hard, interval days. "Moderate" days sort of disappear, while easy days get easier and hard days get harder.

Often this is referred to as 80/20 training, with 80 representing the percent of your total miles that are run at a comfortable, relaxed pace. As with other number-based rules, this one has the advantage of being sharply defined and easy to follow. It's rigid, which is helpful to many. It also removes the temptation to do too-many medium-hard tempo runs.

The Bottom Line: Your training shouldn't follow a flat line. It should have ups and downs--days when you stress yourself, and days when you recover. A periodized 80/20 program can help you follow this pattern, and the ratio often changes to 85/15 or even 90/10 as you get closer to your goal race.

TRAINING: Taper

Don't Skimp On Your Pre-Race Taper

Hard-training runners should give themselves a serious taper before major races. It doesn't make sense not to. Why rack up weeks of highly-focused training and then not allow your body to recover for a peak race performance?

The taper is so important that it has been thoroughly tested by research studies. Most have reached the same conclusion: You taper best when you reduce your mileage to about 50 percent of your typical training amount. Rest those legs! However, you should not stop doing speedwork. Continue to log some runs at the pace most appropriate for your upcoming race, mile to marathon. Just make sure you do significantly less fast training than your toughest workouts. For example, you might run 2 x 800 meters rather than 6- to-8 x 800 meters.

The longer your race distance, the longer your taper should be. Milers can get ready with three to four days of reduced running. Marathoners will need two to three weeks.

The Bottom Line: Treat your pre-race taper as seriously as you have your training buildup. Hard training stresses both the mind and body, by design. And both need time to recuperate, rebuild, and produce an optimal race performance.

TRAINING: Run-walk

Taking Walking Breaks Is Just Another Form Of Intervals

When we first started running, 50 years ago, all anyone cared about was running farther, and running faster. "Walk" was a four-letter word. It never came up in polite running conversation.

We have a different perspective now. A mix of running and walking are simply one form of interval training. In fact, a run-walk routine is a valuable tool for many runners. It's the best way to start running, to come back from injury, and to continue running as you get older.

Let's be more specific: A run-walk is a workout when you run for X minutes, walk for Y minutes, and then start running again. For example, you might run 4 minutes, walk 1 minute, run 4 minutes, and so on. You can tailor a run-walk to suit your particular needs--running longer, or running faster. Be creative and flexible.

The Bottom Line: We know too many runners who have a mental block against the run-walk system. Get over it. You can adjust run-walk to anything from 5K training to marathon or ultramarathon training. We recommend adding it to your workout toolkit.

TRAINING: Positive Psychology

Talk Yourself Up. Just Be Sure To Use Good Grammar

All runners want to improve their mind. There are books and articles titled "Brain Training," high-tech cranial stimulation devices, and many techniques intended to make you tougher and more resilient. Visualization and self-talk are particularly popular.

Visualization refers to mental pictures you create to empower your actions. If you're training for the Boston Marathon, you visualize yourself cresting Heartbreak Hill and running strongly towards downtown Boston. You don't do this once. You do it dozens of times in your Boston training. Repetition is the key.

A recent study in the Journal of Sports Sciences added a new wrinkle to positive self-talk: Grammar makes a difference. British performance experts showed that there's a better way than telling yourself: "I am strong, and I can finish this race." Instead, use the "you" pronoun: "You are strong, and you can finish this race." This is what your parents and coaches have said-- "You can do it"

--so it seems to spark an existing brain connection.

The Bottom Line: It's important to train the heart muscles and leg muscles, but also crucial to train your positive-thinking pathways. Strong visualization and self-talk practice is easy, and can prove highly effective.

NUTRITION: Carbohydrates

Your Key Source Of High-Octane Fuel

No macro-nutrient is more loved and also despised than carbohydrates. It's easy to see why. Research convincingly shows that carbohydrates are the best source of easy-to-burn calories when you're running hard. (See the next section for a review of the ketogenic diet for runners.) For proof, we need look no farther than the exceptional Kenyan distance runners. They receive almost 70 percent of their daily calories from carbs, including cup after cup of steaming tea laden with sugar.

At the same time, our supermarkets and convenience stores are overflowing with ultra-processed high-carb "junk foods." These are likely responsible for the global obesity crisis, along with an epidemic of inactivity.

While distance runners can afford to eat the occasional processed-carb snack, it's much smarter to choose carb-dense whole foods like grains, veggies, fruits, nuts and legumes. These will contain the ready-to-run energy you need, along with a full complement of healthful vitamins, minerals, fiber, phytochemicals, and more.

Bottom line: Carbohydrates are not the problem with our modern diet. The problem is too much processing, too much sugar, and too much fat. While some runners might be overly sensitive to carbs, most of us perform our best on high-carb whole foods.

NUTRITION: Proteins

You Don't Need Much, But Aim For Some At Every Meal

Runners talk a lot about protein, especially after a hard effort on the roads or a gym workout. However, there's little reason for concern. In the modern Western world, just about everyone gets enough protein. Vegan or vegetarian? Not a problem, according to a 2014 analysis in Nutrients.

In fact, if you're consuming enough calories to maintain a healthy weight, you're very likely getting enough protein. Runners need more calories, and eat more calories, so their protein intake is generally high. Use "protein shakes" only if you enjoy them.

Today, most sports nutritionists advise that we aim for a modest amount of protein at every meal. That can mean: yogurt, a tofu scramble, a peanut butter sandwich, a glass of milk, a handful of nuts, or a small piece of chicken or tuna mixed into cooked grains and veggies. Many ethnic cuisines provide sufficient healthy protein through different (and tasty!) food combinations. Senior runners and high-mileage runners may need slightly more protein than others.

Bottom line: Try to consume a little protein at every meal. Your body--especially the exercising body--likes to have a steady supply of amino acids to assist the daily renewing and rebuilding process.

NUTRITION: Fats

You Don't Need To Avoid Fats--Just The Unhealthy Ones

For several decades, many runners regarded fats as the hidden enemy in their diet. Carbohydrates were good, but fats were evil, because they contained a dense supply of calories without providing fuel efficiency. Now we know different--not just we runners, but everyone.

Fats aren't dangerous (with the exception of trans fats), perhaps no more than carbs and protein. The issue is excess calories of any kind, and too little exercise. This is the pernicious combo that causes weight gain, obesity, and related health problems. Even saturated fats are no longer considered a major risk.

Meanwhile, a high-fat diet known as the keto or ketogenic diet has become popular among its avid adherents, including some runners, particularly ultra-runners. Keto fans believe it can help weight-loss efforts, and perhaps even improve endurance performance. There's no evidence of the latter, though there are anecdotal stories.

The Bottom Line: Fats are a necessary part of all diets, and the body needs a certain amount of fats to perform key biological functions. In general, it still appears most prudent to focus your diet on whole grains, colorful fruits and veggies, and monounsaturated oils like olive oil. But don't be afraid to experiment and find what works best for you.

NUTRITION: Hydration

Drink To Thirst. Don't Worry About Small Weight Loss

Runners train hard, and sweat a lot. So it's no surprise that proper hydration has always been a big concern. If you don't stay sufficiently hydrated, you can't race your best ... or even train and function your best.

That said, hydration has often been overemphasized in both our culture at large and among runners. Decades ago, runners were warned to drink enough to avoid weight-loss in training and racing. But this is both impossible and unnecessary. Now top endurance scientists advise that we drink when thirsty, and expect to lose up to 2 percent of body weight. It's not dangerous, and won't make you slower.

You can replace any lost fluids after you stop running. This way you'll also avoid hyponatremia, a potentially fatal condition that results from overdrinking.

The Bottom Line: Drink when you get thirsty, not before. In runs and races that last less than an hour, you generally do not need to drink. In longer runs, including marathons, try to consume 6 to 8 ounces of fluid every 20 to 30 minutes. Choose drinks with a modest amount of sugars (for energy) and electrolytes like sodium and potassium to maintain electrolyte balance.

NUTRITION: Vitamins & Supplements

Insurance? Sure, Go Ahead. Proof? Very Little

Every runner committed to a sensible training program and good injury-prevention strategies--that is, you and us--also wants to aim for optimal nutrition. And nothing could be easier than a multi-vitamin and maybe a supplement or two, right? After all, nutritionists are always yelping about that anti-oxidant or this other crazy-sounding phytochemical.

Taking a pill or two seems the smart approach. Okay, be our guest. But understand that you'll likely end up with expensive, neon-colored, urine. You'll pee away the pill contents, and gain no particular payoff.

Nutrition studies have consistently shown that vitamin, mineral, and supplement pills rarely produce the desired effect. They should work, in theory anyway. But they don't. Your money will go farther and produce better results if you spend it on high-quality, whole foods. Most varied Western diets contain all the nutrients you need, in their healthiest form. That is--as real foods. (For strict vegans, a vitamin B12 supplement is a good idea.)

The Bottom Line: When it comes to nutrition, spend 99 percent of your time planning the best ways to consume a varied, whole-food diet. Pills are popular, but there's little to no evidence that they are effective.

NUTRITION: Plant Diets

Many Vegans And Vegetarians Run Strong. You Can, Too

Every year more and more people, including endurance athletes, turn to vegetarian or vegan diets, which today are often called plant-based diets. Some switch because they believe the diets healthier, some believe them more ethical, and some believe them more environmental.

We'll only comment here on health and performance. Can runners train and race their best on plant-based diets? Absolutely. Scott Jurek and many other ultra-runners have set records on vegetarian diets, and research consistently supports plant-based diets. A 2019 report in Nutrients concluded that plant diets reduce inflammation, increase antioxidants, help maintain a lean body weight, and foster good glycogen storage. As a result, the paper stated: "Plant-based diets may offer performance advantages."

Strict vegans will need to take Vitamin B12 supplements, since B12 is only found in meat, eggs, and dairy. But protein and iron are no longer considered a problem for most vegetarians, according to Harvard Health.

The Bottom Line: There are more plant-based athletes than ever before, and also more performing at the top end of endurance competitions. Plant-based athletes simply need to consume sufficient daily calories from a variety of healthy foods including whole grains, legumes, nuts, seeds, and colorful fruit and vegetables.

NUTRITION: Carbohydrate Loading

Yes, It Works. But Keep It Simple And Effective

Carbohydrate loading has been around for a half century now, and proven effective in countless studies. It's specific to your diet before marathon races. You don't need it for shorter races, even half marathons.

Here's how it works. Your muscles function best on glycogen, which they get from the foods and drinks you consume. Carbohydrates convert to glycogen more efficiently than fats or proteins, so carbs are your friend for several days before a marathon. In the 1960s and 1970s, marathoners often "depleted" their glycogen supply for three to four days in order to "super-compensate" in the following days.

Newer research has simplified the process. You only have to taper your training for three or four days pre-marathon while simultaneously consuming a high-carb diet. Simpler is better, so follow the new approach, not the old way.

The Bottom Line: Several days before a marathon, be sure to reduce your training substantially and focus on carbohydrate foods and drinks. You don't have to stuff yourself with carbs; that could lead to trouble. Just eat foods that are high in carbs but low in fats and proteins: bread, pasta, rice, potatoes, etc.

SHOES: Selection

Buy Your Shoes At A Local Retail Store

With the growth and low prices of Internet shopping, this nugget of Timeless Wisdom is gradually losing market share. But we're here to defend it. To find the best running shoe for you, it's essential to try on several pairs--maybe even four or five. The only place you can do that is at a specialty running store that carries a variety of brands and models.

If you're lucky, the store will also have experienced staff who can guide your selection. They can tell you what shoes their customers have been raving about, and perhaps even match your running biomechanics to an appropriately-designed shoe.

With each shoe you sample, take a short try-out jog down the nearest sidewalk. If a shoe feels like a clunky appendage to your foot, that's not the one you want. Select the shoe that feels the most like an almost-natural extension of your foot.

Bottom line: Buy your new shoes at a specialty running store. Try on a handful, and select the pair that feels most fluid and natural on your feet. (See Benno Nigg, next page.)

SHOES: Brain Smarts

Believe In Comfort And Your Central Nervous System

Runners spent nearly a half century being befuddled by shoe companies. First the companies scared us with specific, technical-sounding problems: Beware of over-pronation ... or under-pronation. Then they produced shoes that supposedly corrected for this issue.

Only the shoes rarely worked as promised.

Meanwhile, one of the most respected researchers in the business kept publishing studies that countered the shoe-company claims: Cushioned shoes didn't actually deliver more cushioning, he concluded, and overpronation wasn't necessarily a bad thing. His name was Benno Nigg, from Canada's University of Calgary.

Finally, in 2015, Nigg put all his ideas together in the British Journal of Sports Medicine. Nigg wrote that every runner's legs and feet followed a "preferred movement path." That way to find your groove was to pay attention to your "comfort filter." In other words, buy the shoes that feel the best on your feet and move the best with your legs.

The Bottom line: Choose shoes that feel natural and comfortable on your feet. These shoes will enable you to run in your uniquely personal manner. You'll achieve your best performance with the fewest injuries. Listen to your body (and brain). Trust yourself to make the right choice.

SHOES: Care and Feeding

Treat Your Shoes Like The Best Friends They Are

Your running shoes are a bit like your car: Treat them well, and they will return the favor. Don't put your damp or wet shoes in the dryer for example; they don't like high heat. They don't like direct sunlight either. Instead stuff crumpled newspapers in your shoes, and let them dry out for several days.

Shoe experts also recommend that you untie your shoes after each use. This allows them to return to their natural shape. It's also a good idea to give your shoes "off days" just as you give your body easy days. This helps the midsole foam to recover. At the same time, running in different shoes is good for your legs.

Don't pull your shoes off over the heel without un-tying. You can repair worn-out soles with shoe goo. But don't do this in place of buying new shoes when you need them.

The Bottom Line: A quality pair of running shoes should last 400 to 500 miles. With good care, you can extend this mileage a modest amount. But don't overdo. It's the midsole that really counts, and when it's time for a new midsole, it's time for new shoes. Period.

SHOES: Gimmicks

Less Is More. Choose A Middle-Of-The-Road Pair

In the 40+ years that have passed since the running boom of the mid-1970s, athletic footwear companies have produced and sold shoes with literally thousands of different technical devices intended to improve your running. Some are supposed to make you faster; some are supposed to prevent injuries; some are supposed to improve shoe life. Few have delivered on their promises.

Today, smart runners follow this rule: Wear the least shoe you can get away with. If you know you are an overpronator, and often troubled by knee pains, okay: Buy a slightly-heavier shoe with a wedge or post designed to prevent overpronation. If this shoe works for you, stick with it. If you need more cushioning, buy a thick, plush shoe.

Otherwise, choose a simpler, lighter shoe that's comfortable and well-constructed. As long as you don't develop injuries, stick with the mid-way shoe. A recent U.S. Army study verified this approach. The most injured soldiers were those who wore minimalist shoes. The second most-injured group wore maximalist shoes. The runners in the middle? They did fine.

The Bottom line: Buy the "least shoe" that works for you. Unless you have a specific biomechanical problem and know that you need extra protection, less is more.

SHOES: Barefoot Running

Better In Theory Than In Practice

When Christopher McDougall's epic adventure book Born to Run hit the best-seller list in 2009, it set off a wave of interest in barefoot running. Actually, the ultra-distance running Tarahumara Indians of Mexico's vast Copper Canyon mostly run in huaraches today. They fashion their rugged footwear from discarded automobile tires.

But McDougall cited a number of experts and studies that cast doubt on the usefulness of conventional running shoes, especially those made with thick cushioning. Evolutionary biologists pointed out that shoes are a recent invention on the human timeline, and paleo runners ran great distances and prospered without Nikes or Adidas.

The story was both mesmerizing and compelling, and thousands of runners decided to give it a try. They ran either barefoot or in various types of super-thin running footwear. A few succeeded; too many got injured. The fad lasted a few years and then gave way to thick, plush shoes constructed of newer, lighter-weight foams. Fads often follow a see-saw pattern.

Bottom line: Our environment has changed over the millennia--that is, we live in a world of hard, sometimes dirty, sharp, and even dangerous surfaces. Ninety-nine percent of runners prefer shoes, and perform better in shoes. Stay in the mainstream.

HEALTH: Your Heart

Keep On Running To Keep Your Heart Ticking

We run for many reasons, perhaps primarily because high-level fitness leads to high-level living on the physical, mental, and emotional scales. For sure, many of us run because we think it will help us build a stronger heart and live longer.

This is mostly true, but it's also complicated. Studies have shown that runners, with their elevated cardiorespiratory fitness, have a 30- to 40-percent lower rate of heart disease than non-runners. In fact, a report in the medical journal Lancet showed that the first 20 runners to break 4 minutes in the mile (since Roger Bannister, 1954) lived an average of 12 years longer than their contemporaries.

That said, the risk of a heart attack actually increases while you are running. We believe runners should review a CPR video at least once a year as a refresher. You could save the life of a runner friend, or fellow race participant.

The Bottom Line: Running is good for your heart, but doesn't guarantee protection from heart disease or a heart attack. Pay attention to all symptoms, and see a doctor if you have any unusual chest pains, shortness-of-breath, or other worrisome signals. Eat healthy too; that can make a difference.

HEALTH: Your Skin

Protect Yourself From Environmental Onslaughts

Running is great for so many areas of your health and life. This doesn't apply to your skin, however. The biggest issue is exposure to solar radiation, and risk of skin cancer. Runners get more skin cancers than sedentary "Game of Thrones" fanatics. Most are non-malignant basal-cell cancers, but they still require monitoring and treatment.

So make good use of sunscreen when you run in bright daylight hours, okay? Pick the sunscreen you tolerate the best and are most likely to use regularly. Put it on your face, ears, neck, shoulders, arms, and legs. Also, consider a hat/visor, and run in the early-morning or late afternoon if those hours work for you. Schedule yearly checkups with a dermatologist.

Sun, wind and "weathering" age the skin, causing wrinkles and splotches you'd rather not have. Basic skin care helps. Use moisturizers as necessary, and avoid long, hot showers in dry winter weather.

The Bottom Line: Running brings a lot of health benefits, but great skin isn't one of them. Your skin takes a beating when you run outdoors in the sun, in the cold, and on windy days. Use sunscreen, moisturizers, and other basic skin-care protection.

HEALTH: Pain Killers

Aim To Run Without Pain And Without Pain Killers

We runners suffer from irregular bouts of aches and soreness. This is a fact of life that's undeniable. However, most running aches come from the soft tissues--muscles, tendons, and ligaments--and they disappear with rest. Don't keep running through these pains. Yes, it's great to be motivated and set ambitious goals. But it's even better to rest and recover from injuries rather than pushing through.

Just about every runner relies on a few NSAIDs (over-the-counter pain killers) from time to time. Okay, we get that; it comes with the turf. But don't use them for long periods, and don't let them become a normal part of your training routine. NSAIDs can have side effects on the heart and kidneys, while increasing stroke and blood-pressure issues.

It's far smarter to rest and practice physical therapy than to keep running and risk a more major problem. Try a cross-training workout that doesn't stress your knee, calf, ankle or foot. When you return to running, adopt a comfortably shorter-stride.

The Bottom Line: Don't misuse NSAIDs to fight common running aches or soreness. Take several days off, switch to cross-training for a time, and run shorter and easier until the soreness resolves.

HEALTH: Immunity

When To Run With A Cold, And When Not To

In general, running boosts your immunity. It makes you more resistant to colds and flu, and--believe it or not--even increases your body's reactivity to a flu vaccination. That's right: High fitness boosts the benefits you get from a flu shot.

None of this means that runners don't catch colds and the flu. Of course, we do. We're susceptible to all the same germs and viruses as everyone else, especially those in planes, workplaces, and other public environments. Like everyone else, runners need to practice good hygiene (hand washing!) to avoid contamination.

Several studies have also shown that runners are more susceptible to colds in the days after running a marathon, or when over-trained. So be especially careful when ou have been pushing yourself hard. Also, limit your running, or stop entirely for several days, when you have a fever and/or chest congestion. You can continue running moderately if you have a run-of-the-mill head cold with sniffles and nasal blockage.

The Bottom Line: You know you should respect injuries and overtraining. Pay just as much attention to colds and respiratory illnesses. Losing a few days of training, or even a week, won't disrupt your fitness plan. Health first!

HEALTH: Weight Loss

Find A Way To Trim Calories And Run More

Literally millions of people have used their running programs to help themselves lose weight. Notice we said "helped." It takes more than regular running. Nutritionists almost universally believe that takes calorie-cutting, and not just running, to produce successful weight loss.

That's because running burns only about 100 calories per mile. (A more exact formula is .75 x your-weight-in-pounds equals calories-burned-per-mile.) That doesn't stack up very well against a typical fast-food meal with a burger, fries, and a shake (more than 1000 calories). And you can consume that 1000-calorie meal in about 15 minutes--a time that's equivalent to only 100 to 150 calories that you would burn in the same 15 minutes

So don't expect a weight-loss miracle simply because you're out there running most days. Be sure to also count your calories. In particular, cut back on the biggest offenders in the typical Western diet: many fast foods, pizza, fried chicken, and other high-fat, high-sugar processed foods.

The Bottom Line: To lose weight, eat fewer high-calorie meals, and run more. This wholistic approach will produce a negative energy-balance, which is what you need for healthy weight loss.

HEALTH: Weight Maintenance

Run Consistently To Maintain Healthy Weight

While experts dismiss running's contribution to weight loss, they're all in on running as a great tool for healthy weight maintenance. Which is a big deal, because maintenance is more than half the battle. In fact, it's a truism that "losing weight is easy, but keeping it is hard.

In study after study, subjects following diet X, diet Y, or diet Z manage to lose weight for 3 months, 6 months, sometimes even a year. But then the pounds creep back. Unless you have a consistent exercise program that you stick with for the long term. (Important note: It's easier to exercise more at a lower weight, so this helps.)

We know exercise works for weight maintenance thanks to the National Weight Control Registry. This database follows more than 10,000 individuals who have lost an average of 66 pounds each, and kept the weight off for a least 5 years. Ninety-four percent increased their physical activity, mainly walking, to achieve their success.

The Bottom Line: Regular exercise is the most proven way to maintain your weight loss. Often it marks the difference between success and failure. The more vigorous your exercise, like running, the better your outcome.

HEALTH: Overcompensation

Don't Give Back The Calories You've Cut

Given the many benefits of a running program, you'll want to maintain all you can. Of course. To do this, be aware of several pitfalls identified in research studies. In particular, watch out for two forms of "overcompensation." Both can affect your overall energy balance, hence your weight loss and/or weight maintenance.

The first happens when you eat too much after you exercise--often in the first hour after a run. This explains why some runners don't lose weight when they begin running. They feel so virtuous after each completed workout that they "reward" themselves with too many calories. This puts them in positive energy balance rather than the negative balance that cuts pounds.

You can also overcompensate by sitting and recovering too much after a run. Don't spend six hours watching Netflix. Instead, do all the usual stuff: taking a family walk, mowing the lawn, or even vacuuming the house.

The Bottom Line: Be vigilant about possible overcompensation traps. Eat healthy foods, not in large quantities, after your workouts. And don't rest on your laurels by resting on the couch after a workout. Avoid too-much sitting. Stay active.

HEALTH: Fit but Fat

Keep Running Even If You Don't Lose Weight

Some runners lose very little or no weight despite their consistent running. Yep, this can be discouraging. Weight-loss might have been one of your major goals. If you don't achieve it, you could be tempted to quit running. Don't! You can gain virtually all the health benefits of running even if you don't lose weight.

We know this because of research results often termed "Fat but fit." These studies track regular exercisers who remain overweight or even obese despite their running. You would expect them to have the health issues associated with carrying extra pounds.

But, no. On most important health markers, these fat-but-fit individuals ace the exam; they have good cholesterol, good insulin sensitivity, and good blood pressure. Most importantly, they feel good-- optimistic, energetic, involved in their families and communities.

The Bottom Line: Whether you reach your weight-loss goal or not, keep running. High fitness offers many health benefits no matter what the bathroom scale says. (Of course, you should continue trying to lose a few more pounds, but don't get depressed about it, and don't stop running.) Keep moving, keep heating healthy, and stay positive.

HEALTH: Sleep

Make Healthy Sleep A Part Of Your Training Plan

When it comes to choosing between running and sleeping, we say, "Do both." We'll let you figure out the details.

Seriously, though, when runner and writer Christie Aschwanden, wrote the book, *Good to Go,* about recovery techniques, she looked into every trick she could find. And she was only able to collect convincing evidence for one: sleep. Not long ago, some people bragged about all they could accomplish on just five or six hours a night. Now smarter folks have realized this is a short-term approach. Sleep is the new (and legal) drug of choice.

The things that happen while we sleep are quite amazing. Among them: your body releases hormones that assist in tissue repair and growth; other stress hormones drop to a healthy, low level; your immune system releases substances that fight inflammation; your brain refreshes its ability to make good decisions and control bad impulses, like a tendency to overeat and gain weight.

The Bottom Line: Aim for a solid 7 to 8 hours of sleep every night. Try to go to bed at the same time, and wake up at the same time. If all else fails, short naps are a great alternative.

INJURY PREVENTION: Stretching

The Evidence Is Lacking. Stretch Only If It Feels Good

For as long as we've been running, a procession of coaches, trainers, and other advisors have been telling us to stretch regularly to prevent injuries. And it sounds so reasonable. Who doesn't want to be more flexible, both physically and mentally? Who doesn't enjoy the image of a long-striding, super-relaxed, loose and flowing runner?

Unfortunately, decades of research have produced little to no evidence that stretching helps runners avoid injury or improve performance. In fact, the available evidence points mostly in the other direction. Many top distance runners have a tight, constricted, highly-rhythmic stride. It might be that flexibility also means "instability," which no one considers a positive condition for runners.

Our advice: Do stretching exercises, mainly after running, only if you enjoy them and think they keep you healthy. Otherwise, given the limited free minutes in your day, consider other activities such as strength and balance. Both have proven benefits. (See "Strengthening" below.)

The Bottom Line: If you enjoy stretching and believe that it keeps you loose and healthy, go for it. Otherwise, don't expect stretching to produce any injury-prevention or performance-enhancing miracles.

INJURY PREVENTION: Strengthening

Get Stronger. Go Faster And Longer With Fewer Injuries

The case for strength training is better than the case for stretching. Specifically, research has shown that strengthening the lower legs, including the knees, hips, ankles, and surrounding tissues, can make you faster and more injury-resistant. Hill training probably does much of the same.

For knee protection, you want to strengthen the quadriceps muscles and the hip abductor muscles. These are the groups primarily responsible for maintaining knee stability while you run. There are many simple routines, including squats, lunges, and hip-abductor side-walks with resistance bands. You can find these in books and on the Internet.

Some of the best exercises, supported by exciting new research, involve single-leg balance and hopping exercises. The philosophy is simple: You run on one leg at a time, so you should strengthen one leg at a time. In these routines, you do things like standing on one leg while moving your arms and shoulders as if running. Also: Try single-leg heel raises, and hopping forward, backward, and sideways on one leg at a time.

The Bottom Line: Building leg muscle strength can improve your running and injury-protection. Include several standing, one-legged exercises. Start with your body weight only, and build up slowly.

INJURY PREVENTION: Foam Rolling

It Hurts So Good. And It Works

If you're reading these "Timeless Wisdom" pages carefully, you've noticed that we're not big believers in weird tools and gimmicks. Listen to your body, use your brain, keep moving, keep it simple. That's our philosophy.

But there are one or two exceptions, including foam rollers. They seem to work. No doubt that's why so many runners use them on a regular basis ... or at least when pain and soreness intrude. Foam rollers are inexpensive, they let you use your body weight to really dig into problem areas, and published research supports their usefulness.

The biggest and best review paper acknowledged that foam rollers are so new that evidence "is still emerging." Nonetheless, it concluded: "Results suggest that foam rolling may be effective for enhancing joint range-of-motion and pre- and post-exercise performance."

The Bottom Line: Foam rollers represent one of the best ways to practice self-massage. At first you, might feel awkward positioning yourself on the roller, but you'll soon get accustomed to it. You can work areas from your neck down to your feet. Foam rollers are cheap, and there are many variations on the basic theme. Keep one or two around, and use them as needed.

RUNNING FORM: Posture

Run Tall And Straight

Every runner has a unique running form--the way s(he) inclines the upper body, swings shoulders, arms, and hands, and moves the legs and feet. Running buddies can identify each other from a great distance, not by their faces, but by their running form. And runners with every type of running form, not to mention disabilities like leg prostheses, manage to find a way to run their best.

So don't obsess about your form. There are things you can't change, and things you shouldn't bother to change.

That said, there are some basic principles you should follow. The simplest and best: Run tall and straight, with your head above your shoulders above your feet. Don't lean forward excessively, and definitely don't lean forward from the hips. A very modest forward lean is okay, so long as it's a slight lean that makes a straight line from your feet through your hips to your head.

The Bottom Line: Run as relaxed as you can. Don't tense your face or grit your teeth, and don't force your arms back and forth like the pistons of an engine. Let your shoulders hang low and loose, cup your fingers as if you were holding an uncooked egg, and bend your arm about 90 degrees at the elbow.

RUNNING FORM: Stride Rate

Use Comfortably Short Strides

At the 1984 Olympics, physiologist Jack Daniels and his wife, Nancy, teamed up to take a novel measurement. They counted the stride rate of runners from the 1500 meters to the marathon. Result? All took about 180 strides per minute. Of course, these runners were very fast.

We have learned a lot more about stride rate since 1984, and there are two important lessons.

First, over-striding (taking long strides, which results in low stride rates) is inefficient for distance runners, and probably increases your risk of injury. Second, shortening your stride (increasing rate) can improve your efficiency (ie, your best pace), and thereby decrease injury risks.

Your pace influences your stride rate, so 180 shouldn't be everyone's goal. Here's a simple scale that matches pace with optimal stride rate: 5:00 (180); 6:00 (175); 7:00 (170); 8:00 (165); 9:00 (160); 10:00 (155); and so on. These correlations are not exact or scientific, but they make a good guide.

The Bottom line: Run with a comfortably short stride that emphasizes stride rate over stride length. Don't lift your knees too high. Imagine that you are "skimming" down the road.

RUNNING FORM: Arm Swing

Don't Pump Your Arms Like Locomotive Pistons

We hate all those TV advertisements where the big-bucks companies hire a New York City model to pretend she's a runner. (We love that they think running is a great metaphor for an energized, productive life. We do, too.) The problem is that these runners, and/or the directors of the ads, think that you should run by pumping your arms vigorously in front of your body.

You don't run with the arms. You run with the legs. (You've probably noticed this already.) That means you want every bit of available oxygen to go to your legs, which need it desperately. If you also pump your arms hard, they will also require more oxygen. That's wasteful.

Your arms should counterbalance the legs, but move as little as possible. They shouldn't produce excessive motion or "noise." Let them hang loosely at your sides and move gently back and forth. They will also move slightly across your torso, but try to limit this motion. If you think about running "quiet" with your arms, that will probably work well.

The bottom line: Do not thrust your arms forward with the thought that you will simultaneously launch yourself forward. You won't. You'll just waste energy.

CROSS TRAINING: Core Training

Pay Some Attention To Total-Body Fitness

If you were training for the next Olympic Marathon, you'd want your body to look like a Kenyan's: small, lean, super-low body fat. That's what it takes to run a 2:02 marathon. However, you're probably not aiming for the Olympics, and you ought to choose a different path.

There's very little evidence that core-training makes you faster or prevents injuries. But it can produce a stronger, more-balanced body, and we think that's good enough. Simple exercises like the plank and bridges take little time, and should be part of everyone's routine. Equally basic one-legged exercises enhance balance and movement patterns you use while running; remember, you run on only one leg at a time.

The upper body doesn't contribute much to your running. While the arms counterbalance the legs, distance runners want as little upper-body motion as possible. Spend your time working on muscles and joints from the hips to the ankles; that's where you'll get the biggest payoff.

The Bottom Line: The best core-training exercises are the ones that strengthen the connection between your core and your lower body. Don't worry much about the upper body. Focus on balance and functional running movements--the stuff you actually do while running.

CROSS TRAINING: Recovery

Get Off Your Legs, But Don't Overcook Your Workouts

Cross training represents the biggest change in runner training in the last 100 years. Once runners just ran, and maybe lifted a few weights. Now they use cross-training to give their legs a much-needed recovery while still doing a fitness-enhancing workout.

Many runners wisely choose to log their normal miles on three, four, or five days a week, but to cross-train on the other days. You gain the most-effective recovery cross-training when you opt for a non-pounding exercise: rowing, seated bicycling, strength-training, an easy elliptical workout, or anything in the water. (See "Performance Cross Training" below for an alternative approach.)

A day of recovery cross-training serves several important purposes. For one, it gives your legs a rest, so you can train harder the next day. It also decreases your chances of an overuse injury. It might introduce you to the sport of triathlon. At the very least, many runners enjoy the variety.

The Bottom Line: Be sure to include several recovery cross-training days in your weekly schedule. They can help you increase fitness and decrease injuries. Select workouts like swimming and seated bicycling that don't pound the legs.

CROSS TRAINING: Performance

Alternative Ways To Get Faster

While cross-training is most often used for recovery, smart runners know how to adapt cross-training to improve their race times. They use various intense workouts to actually boost performance. These sessions are particularly helpful for often-injured, low-mileage runners who want to avoid too-much hard pounding on roads and tracks.

Instead, they log high-cardio workouts on bikes, ellipticals, and other devices that allow for intense efforts without pain and muscle-bone stress. Standing bicycle sprints, intense elliptical workouts, and sweat-producing step-climber sessions are most productive, because they are most similar to running. That is, they put the body in a standing position.

When opting for performance cross-training, be sure not to overcook your program with too-many hard workouts, ie, both running and non-running. You can't pile one on top of the other. Limit most of your running to relaxed efforts, and then hammer on your cross-training days.

The Bottom Line: Cross training isn't only for recovery; low-mileage runners often use it to improve performance. They mostly do hard interval efforts of 20 seconds to 5 minutes. Start gradually and build the number of repeats you perform. Standing exercises beat seated exercises, provided they don't create pain or injury.

WEATHER: Heat

Run Less, Run Slower, Stay Positive

We wish we could do something to make your hot, humid summer runs easier. (And our own, too.) But there's no simple solution. You can wear more in winter; you can't wear less than almost nothing in summer.

The most important strategy: Adjust your expectations. No one can run as long and fast at 90 degrees as they can at 50. So don't try. Learn to settle for what's reasonable. Go shorter, go slower, and give yourself a pat on the back. On some days, you might have to add 30 seconds per mile, or even more, to your pace. If you need a silver lining, here's one: Studies have shown that even slow hot-weather running increases your fitness by boosting your blood-plasma volume.

Summer is a great time to exercise indoors with air conditioning. Outdoors, run as early as possible, seek shade, and hydrate when you need more fluids. Consider adding more swimming and bicycling workouts to your routine.

The Bottom Line: Stay calm, and moderate your expectations by giving yourself permission to run less and run slower. Summer training and racing can get discouraging, so maintain your optimism. Fall will come. When it does, you'll run both easier and faster.

WEATHER: Cold

Dress Well, In Layers, And Enjoy

Cold--even frigid--weather doesn't present an obstacle to modern-day runners, given all the gear options available. In fact, veteran runners prefer cold days to icky, sticky summer heat and humidity. High-body temperature and dehydration are major running issues. Wearing a few extra ounces of clothing on your legs and torso are not.

The biggest winter issue is wind, so dress in layers that include a breathable t-shirt, a warming middle layer, and a windbreaker jacket of some kind. All should be lightweight, especially the windbreaker. That way, you can take it off and tie it around your waist as necessary. Cold weather also demands good head and ear coverings, and gloves or mittens. (And sometimes below-the-belt protection for men.)

Be sure to adjust your clothing to avoid excessive sweat as you run. Sweat will evaporate and could chill you if the temperature drops or the wind direction (or your run direction) changes. Avoid it by adjusting your clothing as you run. We recommend a windbreaker with a full front zipper. Zip up when you face the win; zip down with the wind at your back.

The Bottom Line: Don't sweat the cold. Dress in layers, cover exposed areas, and stay alert to changing conditions.

SAFETY: For Women

To Run Safe, Run Smart And Well-Prepared

We wish it weren't true, but women continue to face safety issues when running. Not only that, but it happens everywhere--in all countries and cultures. And it's not going away soon, as there are no simple solutions.

So, women, take care of yourselves. Listen to your intuition. If something doesn't feel right, it probably isn't. Change streets or change the time of day when you run. Carry a smartphone to call for help, or take pictures of a license plate.

Wear some sort of ID tag, and bright, reflective clothing so you are easily seen. Always let someone know your route, and when you expect to be back. If running alone, ditch the headphones. You need all your senses.

Run in areas where others are running, walking, and cycling. Avoid narrow streets or alleys, or places where you're the only one in sight. Whenever possible, run with someone else--male or female.

The Bottom Line: Be proactive. Plan your runs with an eye towards safety. If all else fails to stop an attack or harassment, scream, kick, bite, or sing at the top of your lungs. And badly!

SAFETY: Road Smarts

Run Conservatively, And Live To Fight Another Day

Runners don't win battles with motor vehicles, obnoxious drivers, bicycles, or bad weather conditions. Run conservatively at all times, and pay attention to your surroundings. We know you like your earbuds and the tunes, but we'd rather you finish your runs in one piece.

On the roads, run facing traffic, ie, on the left-hand side of the road. Seek out roads with few cars and/or wide, smooth shoulders. Even better: If possible, run in parks with no cars. Choose parks and paths that are widely used by other exercisers--runners, cyclists, walkers. They are your best protection. Whenever possible, run with a friend, especially on long trail runs.

At dawn/dusk and in darkness, wear reflective gear and flashing lights (on your head, chest, or waist), and pay even greater attention to cars. You can see them more easily than drivers can spot you. Don't wait for a car to swerve; make the first move yourself. This isn't a game; it's your life

The Bottom Line: Run conservatively. You are your own first line of defense. Be smart, particularly in the dark, in places you aren't familiar with, and in bad weather.

LIFETIME RUNNING: Consistency

To Stay The Course, Choose Moderation In Most Things

Running makes you feel great on a daily basis--while you're out on the roads and trails, or certainly afterwards. But we believe every runner should deliberately aim for a lifetime of happy, invigorating miles. To get there, the smartest path forward is: be consistent, stay disciplined, practice moderation most of the time.

Sure, you should try to qualify for the Boston Marathon if you want. Or enter an ultramarathon. These may require that you push hard on certain days, maybe for months. Nonetheless, running is full of opportunities; you should sample many.

Yet the big goal should always be healthy lifetime running. You don't need to do weekend 20-milers, or midweek speed on a track. Run happy and relaxed three or four times a week--that's the ticket. For variety, change up your pace a bit every now and then, and don't shy away from challenging hills.

The Bottom Line: Listen to your body and brain. Both are exquisitely tuned to tell you when to run more, and when to run less. Set high standards, but also cut yourself a break when necessary. Don't be rigid; don't aim for extremes. Run moderate, happy, and healthy.

LIFETIME RUNNING: Starting Over

It's Gonna Happen. It's Gonna Be Ugly. So What?

At some point, you'll stop running. You'll break an ankle in a car accident, change jobs and cities, get pregnant, or start a midlife graduate-school program. Things will be so new, jumbled, and confusing that you'll fall out of your running routine.

When life stabilizes, you'll want to start again. Unfortunately, this will be difficult, discouraging, and maybe even depressing. You won't have much time, and with each halting stride, you'll remember the days when you were younger, fitter, lighter, faster, and smoother. You'll wonder: What's the point? Why am I doing this?

Don't let these questions deter you. Of course, you're not the person you were a month, year, or decade ago. Tempus fugit. And none of us can match its pace. But here's the important question: What kind of person do you want to be from this day forward? (A bit of good news: Your running will feel better again in a couple of weeks. It just won't come quickly.)

The Bottom Line: Every return to running will be difficult. So what? Have modest expectations, and keep moving forward, because that's the positive, optimistic, and vigorous way to live. Any other choice is simply unacceptable.

MOTIVATIONAL QUOTES

Who doesn't love a good quote? We all need a little inspiration in our lives, a daily reminder of why we do what we do. Quotes fill that need. You'll find quotes on calendar pages, crossword puzzles, memorial statues, and such. They can pay homage to a subject or person, or just support us through our tough times-- what the shrinks call "motivational psychology."

Many great quotes are short: "To thine own self be true." Others are long, like whole chapters of the world's major religious tomes. Either way, great quotes serve the same purpose. They help us to see--directly, clearly--that which we may already realize but don't often enough stop to contemplate. Great quotes freeze us in place for a moment, and force us to think hard.

The quotes on the following pages are tried, true, and beloved. They don't all come from the mouth or writings of great runners. Some come from philosophers, world leaders, playwrights, even comics. They, too, recognize how daily inspiration keeps them focused on their quests. Words are powerful. Words help us gather our strength and rise to the challenge, or perhaps to see something in ourselves that we wish to change. They keep us on the path.

"Bid me run, and I will strive with things impossible."

—*William Shakespeare*

"No one can say, 'You must not run faster than this, or jump higher than that.' The human spirit is indomitable."

—*Sir Roger Bannister*

"When a person really desires something, all the universe conspires to help that person to realize his dream."

—*Paulo Coelho*

"The will to win means nothing without the will to prepare."

—*Juma Ikangaa*

THE HUMAN SPIRIT: Victory

"They can conquer who believe they can."

–Virgil

"Knowing is not enough; we must apply. Willing is not enough; we must do."

—*Johann Wolfgang von Goethe*

"Be kind whenever possible. It is always possible."

—Dalai Lama

"The miracle isn't that I finished. The miracle is that I had the courage to start."

—John Bingham

"Change your life today. Don't gamble on the future, act now, without delay."

—*Simone de Beauvoir*

"Running is the greatest metaphor for life, because you get out of it what you put into it."

—*Oprah Winfrey*

"And now here is my secret, a very simple secret: It is only with the heart that one can see rightly; what is essential is invisible to the eye."

—*Antoine de Saint-Exupéry*

"If you can fill the unforgiving minute with sixty seconds' worth of distance run / Yours is the earth and everything that's in it."

—*Rudyard Kipling*

"Yet that man is happy, and poets sing of him who conquers with hand and swift foot and strength."

–Pindar

"March on. Do not tarry. To go forward is to move toward perfection. March on, and fear not the thorns, or the sharp stones on life's path."

— *Khalil Gibran*

"Go ahead, every once in a while, and jump into that puddle with both feet. It takes conscious thought to keep play in our running."

—*John Jerome*

"There are as many reasons for running as there are days in the year. But mostly I run because I am an animal and a child, an artist and a saint. So, too, are you."

—*Dr. George Sheehan*

"Great is the victory, but the friendship of all is greater."

–Emil Zatopek

"The pessimist sees difficulty in every opportunity. The optimist sees opportunity in every difficulty."

—*Winston Churchill*

"It does not matter how slowly you go as long as you do not stop."

–Confucius

"You can't wait for inspiration. You have to go after it with a club."

—*Jack London*

"It eluded us, but that's no matter. Tomorrow we will run faster, stretch out our arms farther. And one fine morning...."

—*F. Scott Fitzgerald*

"Do what you can, with what you have, wherever you are."

—*Theodore Roosevelt*

"Don't let yesterday make up too much of today."

—*Will Rogers*

"Mind is everything, muscle mere pieces of rubber. All that I am, I am because of my mind."

—*Paavo Nurmi*

"The way to get started is to quit talking and begin doing."

—Walt Disney

"Even when you have gone as far as you can, and you are staring at the specter of self-doubt, you can find a bit more strength deep inside you."

—*Hal Higdon*

"There is only one corner of the universe you can be certain of improving, and that's your own self."

— *Aldous Huxley*

"Success or failure depends more upon attitude than upon capacity. Act, look, feel successful, conduct yourself accordingly, and you will be amazed at the results."

— *William James*

"We may encounter many defeats. But we must not be defeated."

—Maya Angelou

"If you are in a bad mood, go for a walk. If you are still in a bad mood, go for another walk."

–Hippocrates

"Things work out for the best for those who make the best of how things work out."

—John Wooden

"If you are going to win any battle you have to do one thing: You have to make the mind run the body. The body is never tired if the mind is not tired."

—*George S. Patton*

"I've caught a few bad breaks, but God likes me, and I like Him too. My philosophy is: I just put one foot in front of the other, and keep going."

—John A. "Old John" Kelley

"Do not grow old, no matter how long you live. Never cease to stand like curious children before the great mystery into which we were born."

—*Albert Einstein*

"You are never too old to set another goal or to dream a new dream."

—*C.S. Lewis*

"We do not stop exercising because we grow old. We grow old because we stop exercising."

—Dr. Kenneth Cooper

"My grandmother started walking five miles a day when she was sixty. She's ninety-seven now, and we don't know where the heck she is."

—*Ellen DeGeneres*

"Only those who risk going too far can possibly find out how far one can go."

—*T.S. Eliot*

"Do not wait to strike till the iron is hot; but make it hot by striking."

—*William Butler Yeats*

"God has given me the ability. The rest is up to me. Believe. Believe. Believe."

—*Billy Mills*

"Mental will is a muscle that needs exercise, just like muscles of the body."

—Lynn Jennings

"We all have dreams. To make dreams come to reality it takes an awful lot of determination, dedication, self-discipline, and effort."

—*Jesse Owens*

"There is no passion to be found playing small—in settling for a life that is less than the one you are capable of living."

—*Nelson Mandela*

"Our greatest weakness lies in giving up. The most certain way to succeed is always to try just one more time."

—*Thomas A. Edison*

"If you wish to be out front, then act as if you were behind."

—Lao-Tsze

"The most important thing in the Olympic Games is not to win but to take part. The most important thing in life is not the triumph but the struggle."

—*Baron de Coubertin*

"By failing to prepare, you are preparing to fail."

—Benjamin Franklin

"My whole teaching in one sentence is: "Run slowly, run daily, drink moderately, and don't eat like a pig."

—*Dr. Ernst van Aaken*

"Listen to your body. Do not be a blind and deaf tenant."

—Dr. George Sheehan

PAIN: Suffering

"Pain is inevitable. Suffering is optional."

—old Buddhist saying

PAIN: Agony

"Run like hell and get the agony over with."

—Clarence DeMar

"There be some sports are painful, and their labour / Delight in them sets off."

–*Shakespeare*

"To keep from decaying—to be a winner—the athlete must accept pain. Not only accept it, but look for it, live with it, learn not to fear it."

—*Dr. George Sheehan*

"A race is a work of art that people can look at and be affected by in as many ways as they're capable of understanding."

—*Steve Prefontaine*

"The idea is not to beat the other runners. Eventually, you learn that the competition is against the little voice inside you that wants you to quit."

—*Dr. George Sheehan*

"Run the mile you are in."

—Ryan Hall

"If you want to win something, run 100 meters. If you want to experience something, run a marathon."

—*Emil Zatopek*

"If you feel bad at 10 miles, you're in trouble. If you feel bad at 20 miles, you're normal. If you don't feel bad at 26 miles, you're abnormal."

—*Rob de Castella*

"I thought about how many preconceived prejudices would crumble when I trotted right along for 26.2 miles."

—*Roberta Gibb*

"The marathon has everything—drama, competition, camaraderie, heroism. Most joggers can't dream of being an Olympian, but they can dream of finishing a marathon."

—*Fred Lebow*

ABOUT THE AUTHORS

GAIL WAESCHE KISLEVITZ: A rebel in pigtails

I grew up a tomboy, playing in the woods, climbing trees, wanting to be one of the boys--like my older brothers. They ran track at our high school, and I yearned to do what they did. But it wasn't allowed. This was 1967. My high school had no girls' sports programs. Nada. Girls had no place in sports prior to Title IX. The heck with that!

I'm the type, if you tell me I can't do something as simple as running--something so free, natural, mystical and magical to me--well, you'd better get out of the way. So one night when I was 16, under cover of darkness, I laced up my Keds, and took our family dog Tina out for her evening stroll. We ran around the block together. It was maybe a half-mile. It seemed like forever.

But I returned home utterly transformed. I was thrilled, exhilarated. And since that first time--the night I "discovered" running--I have never stopped. I have run through my children's births, growths, and the births of their children, through two bouts with cancer, and through much more. Running has become my best friend, my passion, my health, my mental therapy, and my religion for 52 years.

Recently, I attended my fiftieth high-school reunion. One of the men suggested that a group of women stand up--we who had not been permitted to play sports in high school, but later found our chosen sport.

As I stood and looked around, I felt like crying. With some sadness, but mostly joy.

AMBY BURFOOT: Every mile is a gift

In 1980, I returned home from a Runner's World work weekend to discover an empty house: no wife, no 3-year-old boy. Strange. I called my mother-in-law. "Now I don't want you to be worried," she began. I gulped hard.

My son was in the hospital with a lung infection that didn't respond to treatment, and had some characteristics of Legionnaire's Disease. Dan got sicker by the day. For three weeks, my wife and I took turns sleeping next to him.

When Dan finally rallied, I developed pneumonia. I wasn't as sick as Dan had been, but I sounded like Darth Vader when I breathed. And I had my biggest race of the year coming up--an annual Thanksgiving Day "Turkey Trot" that I have now finished 57 years in a row.

I thought about not running--cough, cough, wheeze, wheeze. But then I reconsidered. I knew I could manage the distance, and that it wouldn't damage my lungs. I still remember my raspy, scratchy breath that Thanksgiving. And the excitement I felt to once again pass under the finish-line banner, no matter how slow.

I've been running for a long time--since 1963. I've had my share of good days, such as winning the Boston Marathon in 1968. But I've had plenty of bad days, too, let me assure you.

And here's what I've learned. You can't "win" every race or every plan. Life is crazy ... and yet wonderful. As I like to say, "Every mile is a new adventure." Also: "Every mile is a gift."